# NATION IN CRISIS

## CONCEPTS IN COMMUNICATION, INFORMATICS & LIBRARIANSHIP (CICIL)

### *General Editor:* S.P. AGRAWAL

| | | |
|---|---|---|
| CICIL-1 | Development of Library Services in India: Social Science Information **S.P. Agrawal** | Rs. 150 |
| CICIL-2 | Development of Documentation in India: Social Science Information **S.P. Agrawal** | Rs. 250 |
| CICIL-3 | UNESCO and Social Sciences: Retrospect and Prospect **S.P. Agrawal** and **J.C. Aggarwal** | Rs. 250 |
| CICIL-4 | INDIANA : A Bibliography of Bibliographical Sources **M.K. Jain** | Rs. 200 |
| CICIL-5 | Dimensions of Library and Information Science: Kaula Festschrift **V. Venkatappaiah** (Eds.) | Rs. 600 |
| CICIL-6 | Book Numbers: Some Indian Methods **M.P. Satija** and **S.P. Agrawal** | Rs. 100 |
| CICIL-7 | National Policy for University Libraries in India: Problems and Perspectives **N.B. Inamdar** and **L.S. Ramaiah** (Ed.) | Rs. 250 |
| CICIL-8 | Media Utilisation for the Development of Women and Children **B.S. Thakur** and **Binod C. Agrawal** | Rs. 150 |
| CICIL-9 | Terrorism: An Annotated Bibliography **Susheela Bhan** (Ed.) | Rs. 275 |
| CICIL-10 | Transnational Library Relations: The Indo-American Experience **M.B. Konnur** | Rs. 175 |
| CICIL-11 | Geography of Marketing and Commercial Activities in India (Documentation on Research Information) **R.S. Dixit** | Rs. 130 |
| CICIL-12 | Information India 1988: Global View **S.P. Agrawal** and **J.C. Aggarwal** | Rs. 200 |
| CICIL-13 | Women's Education in India: Historical Review, Present Status and Perspective Plan **S.P. Agrawal** and **J.C. Aggarwal** | (in press) |
| CICIL-14 | Cultural Communication in India: Role and Impact of Phonograms **J.M. Ojha** | (in press) |
| CICIL-15 | Second Historical Survey of Educational Development in India: Select Documents 1985-1989 **S.P. Agrawal** and **J.C. Aggarwal** | (in press) |
| CICIL-16 | Documentation Encyclopaedia of UNESCO and Education **J.C. Aggarwal** and **S.P. Agrawal** | (in press) |
| CICIL-17 | Attitude Towards Information: A Study of Post-Graduate Teachers and Researchers in Social Sciences **N.G. Satish** | (in press) |
| CICIL-18 | Librarianship and Bureaucratic Organisation: A Study in the Sociology of Library Profession in India **P.K. Jayaswal** | Rs. 175 |
| CICIL-19 | Literature Search **K.A. Isaac** | Rs. 150 |
| CICIL-20 | Child Education in India: Index to Scholarly Writings in Indian Educational Journals and Newspapers since independence **S.P. Agrawal** and **Naresh Kanta** | Rs. 100 |
| CICIL-21 | Lok Sabha and Vidhan Sabha Elections in India 1989 & 1990: Process and Results with Comparative Study of Manifestos **S.P. Agrawal** and **J.C. Aggarwal** | Rs. 250 |
| CICIL-22 | Islamic Studies in India: A Survey of Human, Institutional and Documentary Sources **Mohamed Taher** | (in press) |
| CICIL-23 | Panchayati Raj: An Annotated Bibliography **N.B. Inamdar, N.G. Satish** and **Anil Takalkar** | (in press) |
| CICIL-24 | Information India 1989-90: Global View **S.P. Agrawal** and **J.C. Aggarwal** | Rs. 500 |
| CICIL-25 | First Handbook of Psychological and Social Instruments **Udai Pareek** and **T. Venkateswara Rao** | (in press) |
| CICIL-26 | Educational and Social Uplift of Backward Classes: At What Cost and How? Mandal Commission and After **S.P. Agrawal** and **J.C. Aggarwal** | Rs. 275 |
| CICIL-27 | Mass Media and New Horizons: Impact of TV & Video an Urban Milieu **H.R. Trivedi** | Rs. 180 |
| CICIL-28 | Definitional Dictionary of Agriculture **I.C. Gupta** and **S.K. Gupta** | (in press) |

*Concepts in Communication*
*Informatics & Librarianship-29*

General Editor: **S.P. AGRAWAL**

# NATION IN CRISIS

ACHIEVEMENTS, FAILURES AND NON-FUNCTION OF THE GOVERNMENT

A Dictionary Catalogue of Promises and Precepts of the NF Party, Process of Action by NF Government, Public Opinion, Pathways and Corrective Measures

**S.P. AGRAWAL**
**J.C. AGGARWAL**

**CONCEPT PUBLISHING COMPANY, NEW DELHI 110059**

ISBN-81-7022-341-5

First Published 1991



*Published and Printed by*
Ashok Kumar Mittal
Concept Publishing Company
A/15-16, Commercial Block, Mohan Garden
NEW DELHI 110059 (India)

*Lasertypeset by*
Microtech Advance Printing Systems Pvt. Ltd.
H-13, Bali Nagar,
NEW DELHI 110015

# GENERAL EDITOR'S INTRODUCTION

When hearts are heavy, words are few . . .

S.P. AGRAWAL

# CONTENTS

# INTRODUCTION

They say 'Circumstances make the man' . . . 'People get the Government they deserve' . . . 'Ancient India had withstood the calamities'. . . .

**Will she now ? . . .**

Isn't it a *Miracle* that the National Front Government with the effective support of little over hundred members out of its 141 members of Lok Sabha (many dissidents) has survived crisis after crisis, though created of its own creation.

It is for the first time in the history of independent India that a minority and multi-party National Front Government assumed office on December 2, 1989 at 12 noon when President Shri R. Venkataraman administered the oath of office of the Prime Minister to Shri Vishwanath Pratap Singh of the Janata Dal at Rashtrapati Bhavan. Shri V.P. Singh became the eighth Prime Minister of India, taking Smt. Indira Gandhi's terms of 1966-77 and 1980-84 as two separate regimes. Earlier, there had been two non-Congress Prime Ministers – Shri Morarji Desai who was in office from March 1977 to July 1979 and Shri Charan Singh who remained in office from August 1979 to early January 1980.

It is a mark of statemanship (under forced circumstances!) that the B.J.P. and the C.P.I., two major political parties — ideologically poles apart, joined hands to give outside critical support to the National Front Government.

It is also creditable that initially just with half a dozen colleagues, Shri V.P. Singh was able to form a new party and subsequently to weld together other parties and to come out successfully after the elections.

The policy of *consensus* followed by the National Front Government paid rich dividents and its departure in the announcement of the implementation of the Mandal Commission Report put the

Nation in the dark.

All parties are agreed that urgent steps should be taken for the upliftment of the educationally and socially backward classes, but the hasty decision without proper consultation angered the supporting parties.

A perusal of the events indicate that the attitude of the B.J.P. was hardened after the unilateral acceptance of the report of the Mandal Commission.

Quite obviously so. All political parties, after all, have an eye on the vote-bank.

It is interesting – or should one say rather suffocating to review the resignation-game of the N.F. right from inception – resignation of the Chief Minister of State Government, of the Central Ministers, of the Deputy Prime Minister, who was prevailed upon to withdraw resignation when tendered, only to be followed by his dismissal from the government sometime later, and not to be left alone, of the Prime Minister who chose to submit resignation when no one desired him to do so.

Incidentally, it may be recollected that the Janata Dal in the first instance had elected as leader of the Lok Sabha Shri Devi Lal, who was one of the main architects of the Janata Dal – his name was proposed by Shri V.P. Singh and seconded by Shri Chandra Shekhar. However, Shri Devi Lal declining it, proposed the name of Shri V.P. Singh. Shri Ajit Singh, seconded this proposal. Shri V.P. Singh was then unanimously elected the leader of the Janata Dal Parliamentary Party.

Events that followed, however, do not enhance any grace. More so because an impression has been allowed to be created in the minds of the common people that the Members of the Cabinet have to spend most of their time in sorting out inner bickerings, organising rallies and attending to all otherwise sundry functions rather than face the administrative challenges and tackle problems gnawing the nation.

No wonder, therefore, that objectivity in dealing with current issues seems to be an illusion.

Young ones – the future hopes of the Nation, are immolating themselves. It is impulsive . . . or, Are they pushed to the wall . . . , or still, is there more than what meets the eye?

Time will tell; posterity will judge.

Our Mythology tells us that *Sati*, the Divine Consort of *Lord Siva*, did the same when her father *Daksha* somewhat power-intoxicated after becoming *Prajapati-Nayak* tried to act irrationally – and surprisingly getting the cooperation of all lesser gods!

And in this, it appears that high hopes of the people of India have been belied and a very dangerous trend set in.

It is also very unfortunate that people, by and large, are losing faith in the creditability of political parties.

The nation is at risk.

Nonetheless hope is not lost in totality still. The paramount need of the hour is that we put the nation above self and the party, and TOP including VIPs, Leaders especially political leaders of all shades, Senior Bureaucrats, Technocrats, Intellectuals, Journalists, Professionals and Business Magnates *et al* set highest standard of public morality so as to instill it UNTO THE LAST.

## ABRACADABRA

### Promises and Precepts

*I. Resolve*

The National Front is committed to upholding the nation's honour and democratic values, promoting the ideal of secularism and ushering a new social and economic order based on equality and justice.

*II. Vision*

We envision an awakened India, free from poverty, ignorance and exploitation, with total involvement of millions in the struggle for national reconstruction.

*III. The Pledge*

We pledge not merely a replacement of one set of rulers by the other, but an alternative model of governance, based on federalism and decentralisation, institutional accountability, economic equality and social justice, human rights, freedom of communication and access to information for all citizens, and a responsive and responsible administration and through all this ensure the dignity of both the individual citizen and the nation.

### Process of Action

No tangible results.

## ADJUNCT AND OBSERVATION

### Promises and Precepts — General Observations

*I. State of the Nation*

Appalling poverty, glaring inequality and growing destitution of large numbers have rendered India weak and demoralised. The people are discontented and disheartened. Escalating conflicts and an increasing resort to violence engulf large areas in the country. In several places mafia gangs and anti-social elements are fully in control.

Today's India witnesses corruption at the highest level in government and administration: an irresolute government unable to resolve conflicts and maintain even minimal law and order, spiralling prices and man-made scarcities; a currency shrinking in value and a mounting load of foreign debt.

The nation is in a whirlpool of crises — crisis of confidence, crisis of character and crisis of leadership — a fallout of the policies pursued by successive Congress (I) governments and particularly by the Rajiv Gandhi Government in the past five years.

The Rajiv Gandhi government, which came into power on a sympathy wave and promised a "Clean government", has scaled new heights in corruption and inefficiency.

Rajiv Gandhi's path to power was marked by the violent deaths of thousands of innocent men, women and children in Delhi and elsewhere in the country. Punjab is now boiling cauldron. What is worse, the spectre of violence has now spread to several other parts of the country. Not a day has passed since his coming to power when scores of innocent citizens have not been massacred in various parts of the country. The communal virus has now assumed the proportions of an epidemic. Atrocities on Scheduled Castes, Scheduled Tribes, and outer weaker sections, as well as women, have multiplied.

Our foreign policy, once lauded for defusing tensions elsewhere in the world has now led to embittered relations even with friendly neighbours like Nepal, Bangladesh and Sri Lanka.

Collusion between an unprincipled government and the unbridled big business has resulted in the prices of essential commodities such as foodgrains, sugar, tea and edible oils sky rocketing at the expense of both the producer and the consumer.

Unemployment of both the educated and the unlettered has reached new heights. Despite tall claims about the elitist New Education policy, the number or illiterates has been increasing and the quality of education deteriorating.

The ruling party, while talking of stability, has itself proved to be the biggest destabilising factor. Divisive forces have been encouraged in sensitive areas to gain short-term partisan ends. The Rajiv Gandhi government, has caused incalculable harm to the institutions of the Republic like the Presidency, the parliament, the judiciary, the CAG and the press. Overnight changes of his own Chief Ministers, frequent Cabinet reshuffles and ceaseless attempts to remove non-Congress (I) governments by foul means, disprove his claim of providing a stable government. The one-party rule at the Centre has been reduced to one-man rule destroying inner party democracy and that one-man rule has proved intolerably incompetent and notoriously corrupt. Bofors, corruption and Rajiv Gandhi are now synonyms. Other brazen scandals such as submarine kickbacks, wasteful expenditure on Westland helicopters, etc., and illegal foreign accounts of proxies of Rajiv Gandhi have rocked our democratic polity to its foundations and endangered the country's security. With conclusive evidence of the involvement of the Prime Minister and his aides in the cover-up of the kickbacks, Rajiv Gandhi has made himself vulnerable to international blackmail. The en-masse resignation of all the opposition MPs from the Lok Sabha, a momentous Bharat Bandh and the rejection of the phoney decentralisation bills symbolise the people's protest against the Government's failures and perversions.

It is against this background that the people of India have been craving for an alternative to the discredited Congress (I). The National Front is a response to this call of our people. The parties that comprise the National Front are deeply committed to the philosophy of national unity, democracy, socialism, securalism and federalism.

In contrast to the Congress (I) misrule, the governments run by the constituents of the National Front have provided dynamic administration, both in the spheres of the development and law and order. Genuine decentralisation of powers to Panchayati Raj institutions, social welfare measures to benefit the weaker sections and women and benefits of farmers, as well as clean and efficient administration, are the outstanding achievements of the National Front Constituent party governments.

To resurrect the nation out of the morass and despondency in which it finds itself today and build a new India, the National Front is offering in this manifesto, a concrete programme and pledges to implement it with all sincerity.

The record of our performance encourages the National Front to approach the people of India with confidence and conviction. We stand united to fulfil our pledge to the nation.

### *II. Wrong Policies*

The National Front believes that mass unemployment, poverty, inequality, ignorance and ill-health are the non-commitant of wrong socio-economic policies pursued by the entrenched ruling elite during the last forty-two years. All these ailments have aggravated in the eighties, more particularly in the last four/five years, when the so-called capital and import-intensive high-tech modernisation of the economy has been attempted to be imposed recklessly and mindlessly.

**Process of Action**

No tangible results.

Regretfully the position is as it were prior to the National Front Government.

## ADMINISTRATIVE STRUCTURE

**Promises and Precepts**

The present administrative system, with its in-built colonial hangover, needs a radical overhaul. A new administrative structure, with new systems, procedures and tools, to promote a new work culture has to be built-up. Administration should be responsive to the needs of the common man and be an effective instrument to achieve radical socio-economic transformation. This would end the alienation between the rules and the ruled and give a new orientation to the role of the civil servant. Honest civil servants at all levels will be protected from harassment and high-handedness. Serious efforts will be made to eliminate red-tape and simplify procedures.

**Process of Action**

No tangible results.

## AGRICULTURE

**Promises and Precepts**

*I. Agriculture*

Land and labour are our most precious assets and their prosperity is correlated. This crucial sector of our economy has not only been neglected for too long but also exploited by an in-built structural disadvantage. The National Front is committed to correct this distortion. It will be our highest policy objective to ensure that the enormous potential of these resources are realised and the corresponding benefits are enjoyed by those who had so far been deprived.

*II. Crop Insurance*

Cultivators will be further protected by insurance of crops and cattle against natural or man-made calamities; an assurance against distress sales by providing godowns; removal of zonal restrictions on the movement of agricultural produce; and a guarantee that the State will purchase crops at assured prices to break market manipulations.

Consolidation of land-holdings will be taken up and completed expeditiously. Holdings of marginal farmers will be grouped into separate blocks for special treatment to increase productivity. The system of levying fixed service charges on irrigation and electricity will be reviewed to make them fair and just, and power will be supplied to farmers at cheaper rate.

Loans up to Rs. 10,000 of small, marginal and landless cultivators and artisans, on October 2, 1989, will be written off, NABARD will provide loans to farmers at concessional rate of interest through cooperative banks.

*III. Inputs and Remunerative Prices*

Remunerative prices to the cultivator and provision of all inputs for agriculture at fair prices will be guaranteed. The prices will be fixed on the basis of real cost of farming by the Agricultural Prices and Costs Commission, which will be strengthened with effective participation of farmers. All prices will be announced before the sowing season. A guarantee that no rural lands are acquired at deferred prices for profiteering by private colonisers or the State and reservation of agro-based industries, including food processing and processing of minor forest produce for cooperative and small scale sector in the rural areas, will guide the agrarian strategy of the National Front.

Marketing Committees, constituted by farmers, will be given liberal credit, transport and warehousing facilities. Elected Karshak Parishads (Farmers' Forums) will be organised at State, District and

Block levels to take up programmes benefiting the farmers. These will be developed into true representative bodies of the farmers.

Export and import of agricultural commodities will be guided by a Commodities Management Board, with effective representation for farmers and consumers, so that the prices of farm produce are not affected adversely. Farmers will be ensured regular supply of inputs and liberal credit facilities.

*IV. Land Reforms*

The National Front will revise the existing laws to bring about equitable distribution of land and other natural resources such as water and make the tiller of the land its owner. All land reform laws shall be included in the Ninth Schedule of the Constitution.

Land Tribunals will be appointed to look into the settled cases of *benami* transfers of land. Surplus land will be distributed among the landless people belonging to Scheduled Castes and Scheduled Tribes.

Two-thirds of our cultivable land is still dependent on rain and large areas, which are potentially cultivable, have remained as wastelands. Priority will be given to provide protective irrigation in the entire rain-fed agricultural areas.

Research in agriculture, animal husbandry, food processing, etc., shall be oriented to make smaller holdings and dry farming economically viable. Emphasis will be on integrative and versatile technology inputs for the small farmer and neglected areas.

**Process of Action**

*I. Land Reforms*

Fifty-five land reform laws passed by various States after 1984 have been included in the Ninth Schedule of the Constitution. A Bill to this effect has been passed in Parliament during the budget session. After inclusion in the Ninth Schedule, these laws cannot be challenged on grounds of infringement of Fundamental Rights guaranteed in the Constitution.

Other measures to bring improvement on the farm front include:

- A new Commission for streamlining Land Revenue administration proposed.

- A Corporation on the lines of NABARD for construction of major irrigation projects.
- Improvement and extension of the crop insurance scheme.

*II. High Powered Committee on Agricultural Policies*

The High Powered Committee on Review of Agricultural Policies and Programmes, chaired by Shri Bhanu Pratap Singh, has recommended that agriculture be given the same facilities and incentives as industry.

In its report, submitted in July 1990 to the then Deputy Prime Minister and Agriculture Minister, Shri Devi Lal, the Committee has said that agriculture and industry should have the same norms, standards and criteria both in fixation of prices and provision of budgetary support, credit, power, transport and export facilities.

As long as it receives the same benefits, agriculture need not be given the formal status of industry, the Committee notes. However, if the bias against agriculture cannot be removed without formalising its status, then it should be given the same status as industry, says the report.

The Bhanu Pratap Singh Committee was appointed by the National Front Government in January to examine the possibility of according agriculture the same status as industry.

The main points of the Committee's report reflect the current thinking in the Agriculture Ministry as embodied in the draft agricultural policy resolution.

There is general agreement among agriculturists that the rural sector has been ignored far too long and the only way to remove poverty, unemployment and economic disparity is to give agriculture the incentives and benefits that it has been denied.

*III. Farmers Welfare*

Addressing a press conference after submitting his report, Shri Singh said the terms of trade must change in favour of the farmer. The emphasis must be on increasing the farmer's productivity and on his welfare.

He said procurement prices of paddy and wheat should be linked to parity prices and must be the sum of a farmer's input costs and his consumer needs. This is the only way to ensure that procurement prices benefit the farmer.

The committee has recommended doubling the present rate of capital formation in the farm sector so that agriculture production doubles within 15 years and achieves an annual growth rate of 4.7 per cent. The growth rate suggested by this Committee is roughly the same as envisaged in the draft agricultural policy.

The committee has also suggested a credit card system for farmers to get loans easily. A farmer's credit status should be determined once and for all and he should be given loans accordingly, rather than go through the tedious process of producing and assessing documents each time, Shri Singh said. In addition, the terms of credit, established decades ago, must change with the times and take into account the increasing costs of inputs, he emphasised.

The committee has come down heavily on the Food Corporation of India and suggested considering of an alternative food security system which is less costly to the exchequer and more beneficial to the poor.

It recommends restoring the farmer's freedom to sell his produce within a price band of lower and upper prices set by the Government. Let farmers put their produce in rural warehouses controlled by the Government only if they want to, Shri Singh said. Otherwise they should be free to sell their produce in the market if they feel that they can get a higher price. However, if prices threaten to go above the upper limit set by the government, then the latter has the right to step in and acquire enough produce to bring prices down.

The report says that direct producer-consumer links should be promoted and suggests whittling down the public distribution system to providing food aid only to the genuinely poor.

It has also recommended that expenditure on major and medium irrigation works be limited only to completing on-going projects for the moment and more attention be paid to minor irrigation works particularly in the eastern states. Drainage should be given the same attention as irrigation.

On land reforms, the committee has suggested that anyone who brings barren land under cultivation should be allowed to keep 50 per cent of that land above the land ceiling limits provided he surrenders the other 50 per cent for redistribution among the landless.

## General Observations

### *Farm Policy*

The Government statement on the Draft Farm Policy released on July

11, 1990 stated that the share of agriculture in the Gross Domestic Product (GDP) came down from 60 per cent in 1950-51 to 30 per cent in the 80s. However, there was marginal decline in the percentage of the population depending on agriculture. In real terms, this number has doubled, from 290 million in the 50s to 580 million today — that is 76 per cent of the population.

The purchasing power of the farmer, in terms of trade as it is called, is down to 87 from 100 in 1965 and in fact a vast majority of wage labour in rural areas do not get a living wage.

The spurt in the rural population over the past three decades has meant that the per capita land available has shrunk. In 1970, there were 70 million land holdings, in 1985, there were 98 million. In other words, the size of the average land-holding has shrunk by 40 per cent to 1.68 hectares. The landholdings, therefore, are highly fragmented.

The policy also points out that while the production of rice, wheat and certain other crops has increased substantially over the years, the production of pulses, oilseeds and cereals has not. Farmers have to be encouraged to diversity into cash crops and other sectors such as fisheries, etc. which will also help in generating capital in rural areas.

(*Indian Express*, July 12, 1990)

## ART AND CULTURE

### Promises and Precepts

The National Front Government will take steps to democratically evolve a National Cultural Policy through encouragement of and respect of different cultural identities and their manifestation. But, the present government has been promoting 'Sarkari Culture' with great fanfare.

The National Front Government will promote classical and folk traditions in arts, crafts, music, theatre, dance, etc., and encourage them through traditional institutions and schools, which evolved and sustained them for hundreds of years. Expensive and ostentatious centrally-sponsored festivals and synthetic *utsavs* will be abandoned in favour of a multitude of local initiatives and talents.

Schemes for giving financial support to artists will be reviewed and strengthened so as to encourage them in their creative pursuits.

A comprehensive National Cultural Policy will be formulated.

**Process of Action**

No tangible results.

## CIVIL LIBERTIES

**Promises and Precepts**

Civil liberties and human rights will be protected and strengthened. The 59th Amendment to the Constitution, the Posts and Telegraphs (Amendment) Bill, and the other laws violative of civil liberties shall be withdrawn. Undertrials shall be safeguarded from harassment. Institution of Executive Magistrates, wherever they exist, shall be dispensed with. The U.N. Conventions against torture and those relating to prisoners and refugees shall be ratified and adopted. Suitable prison reforms will be undertaken on a systematic basis.

**Process of Action**

*Indian Post Offices (Amendment) Bill*

The controversial Postal Bill introduced by the previous Government has been withdrawn. The Bill sought to confer power, on postal authorities to intercept articles in transit in certain cases. It was felt that such a power would seriously interfere with citizens' right to privacy. Individual's right to privacy is further ensured by the assurance given by the Government in Parliament to amend the Indian Telegraph Act so as to do away with telephone surveillance.

## COMPANY LAW AMENDMENT

**Promises and Precepts**

Company Law will be suitably amended to curb malpractices indulged in by private corporate sector, particularly family managements.

**Process of Action**

No tangible results.

# CORRUPTION

## Promises and Precepts

### *I. Curbing Corruption*

Corruption not only demoralises the people but also robs the poor as plan priorities and delivery to target groups are distorted. The National Front reiterates its firm conviction that with the transformation of the administrative set up, corruption will also be curbed. An institution of Lok Pal will be created at the Centre and Lok Ayuktas will be introduced in States and strengthened where they exist. The purview of the Lok Pal and Lok Ayukta will be expanded to include the highest political offices in the country. It will also be laid down that the Lok Pal, Lok Ayuktas, the Comptroller and Auditor General (C & AG), the Chief Election Commissioner and the Chief Justice of India will hold no public office after retirement. All elected representatives to legislatures and Zilla Parishads will be required to periodically declare their assets and incomes for scrutiny by an appropriate authority.

## Process of Action

On December 29, 1980 the Law Minister Shri Dinesh Goswami introduced the Lokpal Bill in the Lok Sabha as a part of the fulfilment of the National Front's promise to provide for cleaner public life in the country. The Bill makes an important departure from the Bills introduced earlier on the subject by bringing even the Prime Minister within the jurisdiction of the Lokpal.

Introducing the Bill, the Minister pointed out that it had a chequered history going back to 1968. Having studied the interim report of the Administrative Reforms Commission in 1966 on the subject and all the four Bills which were introduced in Parliament earlier, the Government had come to the conclusion that legislation for setting up the institution of Lokpal was imperative.

It was necessary to combat the problem of corruption at higher political levels. In the interest of democracy it should be the endeavour of every public functionary at the top political level to maintain high standards of public morality.

The present Bill seeks to set up a Lokpal institution, consisting of a chairman and two members. Only persons who have been judges of the

Supreme Court will be eligible for appointment of this body. It has been proposed that it create greater assurance of justice and fairplay in the minds of all, the jurisdiction of Lokpal should cover the Council of Ministers, including the Prime Minister.

It is also proposed that in the case of Ministers the authority to decide on the recommendations of the Lokpal would be the Prime Minister; and in the case of the Prime Minister the House of the People as ultimately the political functionaries are responsible to the people through their representatives. To ensure that this institution functions with utmost objectivity and independence, it is provided that their salary, and other conditions of service, including removal from office, shall be equivalent to those of the Chief Justice of India in case of the chairman, and judges of the Supreme Court in case of the other members.

After the Minister had moved the Bill, a section of BJP and Janata Dal members demanded that the provisions of the Bill be made applicable with retrospective effect. Shri Madan Lal Khurana (BJP) in this context explained how changes in the election law were made applicable with retrospective effect in case of former Prime Minister Indira Gandhi.

The Minister explained that the Bill provided that the Lokpal would not inquire into any complaint if it was made after the expiry of five years from the date on which the offence mentioned in the complaint had been committed. This had been done as they could not keep the issue open for all times to come.

Minister said it was a part of the series of promises made by the National Front to provide for a clean political life. They aimed to fulfil these promises in full.

**Public Opinion**

Madhukar S. Heble, in an article 'How the Corrupt Flourish' has stated "How are the Augean stables to be cleaned? Will the institution of the Lok Pal, if and when it comes into existence, improve matters by placing a curb on ministerial corruption? Going to our experience of the Lok Ayukts in several States, one fears not. In many, if not most cases, the Government has treated the posts of Lok Ayukt and Up Lok Ayukt as sinecures to be conferred on superannuated Chief Secretaries and High Court judges as rewards for long, undistinguished and pliant service. Will the person occupying the Lok Pal's office be any different?"

(*Indian Express*, July 12, 1990)

In the words of Prof. S.R. Maheswari, "In short, the Bill is an improvement on the earlier ones only in two respects: its jurisdiction covers the Prime Minister; and it visualises a plural membership body. Virtually, in all other respects, it is the National Front's edition of the Rajiv Gandhi's Lok Pal Bill of 1985. The Bill, if passed in its present form, is unlikely to provide a machinery which will be efficient in curbing a cancerous growth in the Indian society and polity."

(*Hindustan Times*, March 27, 1990)

*II. Bofors*

**Promises and Precepts**

The National Front stands firmly for dismantling the nexus between politicians and vested interests and to eradicate the all-pervasive corruption. It will track down the kickback funds generated in Bofors and other deals and slashed away in foreign banks. The funds will be restored to the national and the guilty will be punished.

**Process of Action**

The CBI has filed FIR against persons allegedly involved in the Bofors guns, the HDW submarines and the A-320 airbus purchases.

**Public Opinion**

AICC-I spokesman M.J. Akbar said on August 29, 1990 that revelations made by *Independent* of Bombay had exposed . . . that all through the Bofors controversy it was not understood as to how as Finance Minister Shri Singh could distance himself from the whole process. His consistent answer was that all he did was that he had initiated the deal and had at no point of time was involved in negotiations.

The *Independent* has however made clear what role Shri Singh had played. The revelations made by the Independent clearly proved that Shri V.P. Singh had been participating in the discussions and negotiations from the very beginning. "I also want to state that he was in fact sent with an official brief on the subject when he went to Stokholm and the evidence before the JPC reportedly showed his continuous involvement", Shri Akbar alleged.

He further said why did Shri Singh lie about his involvement in the Bofors negotiations? The basic question was what did he have to hide?

He said from the very beginning we had been saying that a selective look at the Bofors papers led to unnecessary questions and confusion. There was a very simple way of finding out the whole truth. All the papers, we have been saying again and again, should have been placed before the country "You have all the government files lay them before the country", he demanded.

Asked why the Congress leaders had not exposed Shri Singh earlier and why they waited till the *Independent* published the story, Shri Akbar remarked that Congress Government was not so irresponsible. "It was a secret of the Government and under the Cabinet system of Government no secret could be leaked out. The Government must react on the *Independent* report".

He also said that there would be a deafening silence on the part of BJP, Janata Dal and the CPI-M on the *Independent* report who were hysterical on Bofors deal.

(*Hindustan Times*, August 29, 1990)

## DEBT : FOREIGN AND INTERNAL

### Promises and Precepts

*I. Foreign Debt*

The National Front shall restore to the nation its dignity and confidence by achieving self-reliance in the economy. The National Front's policies will be directed towards freeing the country from indiscriminate and highly expensive technologies, the humiliating burden of fast escalating foreign debt and the abject dependence on multinational corporations.

*II. Indebtedness*

The Congress(I) policy of dependence on foreign technology has resulted in rapid and stupendous increase in foreign debt which has already exceeded Rs. 100,000 crores.

The burden of internal debt too has reached a menacing level of Rs. 200,000 crores so that interest payments have already become the most important component of non-plan expenditure of the government. The country is fast heading towards bankruptcy and debt trap.

The National Front will alter these policies and resist the pressures which have led to such an excessive debt burden. There will be severe and effective controls on deficit financing.

**General Observations**

Internal debt, which was Rs. 96,505 crore at the beginning of the Seventh Plan (1985-86) rose to Rs. 238,096 crore at the end of the plan (1989-90), while external debt (at the prevailing exchange rate) rose from Rs. 35,725 crore to Rs. 80,122 crore between these two periods.

(*Parliament Question-Answer*, August 23, 1990)

## DEMOCRATIC RIGHTS

**Promises and Precepts**

*I. Democratic Rights*

We declare our resolve to extend the democratic rights of our people.

*II. Electoral Reforms*

The Indian State cannot be rejuvenated and made to play its appointed role in social transformation unless it also steps in to combat the growing nexus between the big money, mafias and the politicians. The National Front will urgently implement the long-pending proposals for public financing of elections to reduce money power, regular audit of party funds and observance by political parties of the rules framed by their respective Constitutions. Contrary to the existing practice, the Election Commission will be appointed in consultation with the Opposition. System of multipurpose photo-identity cards will be introduced. Measures for expeditious disposal of election disputes, holding of bye-elections on time and fresh delimitation will be undertaken. To ensure a continuous inflow of new blood dynamism, devotion, dedication and sacrifice into the arena of public life and service the National Front will introduce the principle that legislators at the Centre and State levels are barred from holding any elected office at the district or the lower levels. Suitable changes will be made in the Anti-Defection Law to prevent its misuse.

Comprehensive Electoral reforms to curb money and muscle power will be urgently introduced.

**Process of Action**

One of the first steps contemplated in this direction is electoral reforms. Three Bills on the subject have been introduced by the Government in Parliament. The Bills, among other things, provide for State funding of elections, change in the mode of appointment of the Chief Election Commissioner and the delimitatioin of constitutencies without increasing their number.

## ECONOMIC TASKS

*See*

Agriculture: Crop Insurance; Inputs and Remunerative Prices; Land Reforms
Company Law Amendment
Debt: Indebtedness
Economy and Development: Black Money; Fiscal Policies and Monetary Controls; Poverty Eradication; Tax Relief to Middle Income Groups
FERA & MRTP
Import-Export Policy
Industrialisation
Institutional Finance
Investment on the People
Labour: Labour Policy
Licensing Policy
Natural Resources and Environment
Price Rise Arresting
Public Sector and Private Enterprise
Research and Development
Right to Work
Sales Tax
Water Management
Wrong Policies of the Past

## ECONOMY

### Promises and Precepts

*Black Money*

Effective administrative and economic measures will be taken to curb tax evasion, unearth black money and check its generation at source.

*Fiscal Policies and Monetary Controls*

Our fiscal policy needs drastic change. A long-term fiscal policy for both direct and indirect taxation will be formulated to increase revenue and curb corruption. It will also be ensured that there is a steady rise in the ratio of direct to indirect taxes.

*Poverty Eradication*

Of all the problems facing India none is as stark as poverty. It is a national disgrace that after four decades of Independence, and implementation of seven Five-Year Plans, more than two-thirds of the population remain illiterate, ill-fed, ill-clothed, ill-housed and in poor health, while the rich roll in extravagance, leading an ostentatious life.

The absolute number of the poor in the country today exceeds the total population of India at the time of Independence. More than one-third of the rural population is unable to find productive and gainful work for most of the year. In the urban areas over 35 million people are on the live register as unemployed — a tenfold increase since 1952. The disparities between the top 10 per cent and bottom 30 per cent of the population have, meanwhile, widened menacingly.

Concentration of wealth, assets and incomes, which has created increasingly steep disparities, shall be reduced to a minimum by introducing structural changes, with a strong political will. Growing disparities in incomes and wealth have led to shocking distortions in planned economic development, created vicious circles of poverty, ignorance and squalour and condemned large sections of Indians to dehumanised living. These disparities will be brought down by dispersal of ownership, whether in industry, commerce or trade, and ceiling on urban property and land or agricultural estates and land-holdings as well as incomes. Rationalisation of direct and indirect taxation will be the other measure towards this end. While reiterating its commitment to planning, the National Front shall use it as an instrument for widening the social base of the economy by expanding the purchasing power of the people and extending the benefit of development to the masses rather than a small class of people and by reducing the regional and sectoral imbalance. The National Front reiterates its belief that without the double process of simultaneous lowering of the ceiling and lifting of the floor, it will never be possible to remove poverty and narrow disparities, whether economic or social.

*Tax Relief to Middle Income Groups*

To provide relief to middle income groups, the exemption limit for income-tax will be raised.

**Process of Action**

With a view to saving foreign exchange for combating the balance of payment crisis, the Government, decided on July 3, 1990 to reduce the foreign travel budget of the ministries by 20 per cent in the financial year 1990-91.

It was also decided to close down the foreign promotional offices of the Government of India.

(*Hindustan Times*, July 4, 1990)

**Public Opinion**

*I. Economy*

*Congress (I)*

In the Lok Sabha on August 7, 1990, Shri Gandhi, Congress (I) claimed that the Congress-I Government had bequeathed a healthy economy to the National Front and the coffers were full and not empty when the Congress-I handed over power in December 1989. During the five years of his Government, Shri Gandhi said, the economy was well managed and the inflation had not touched double digit. Even during the drought year of 1987, he said, the economy was well managed and in 1989, with oilseed, production going down by 23 per cent and despite worldwide inflation, the economy was kept under control by his Government.

But during the past eight months of the NF rule, there had been runaway inflation and the coffers "are now truly empty".

In a broadside against the leftists, Shri Gandhi said he wondered they of all people should support this Government. He told the House that the Congress-I party was not interested in the fall of the NF Government and wished it ran the full five-year term. Nevertheless, he called upon the leftists to do something to influence the Government to bring down prices.

### *CPI*

Shri Somnath Chatterjee, the CPI leader, said this remark was totally unwarranted and Smt. Geeta Mukherjee deputy leader of the CPI group called this the "joke of the century", but Shri Gandhi was unruffled and taunted the Leftists by saying "every time the Prime Minister gets up the crutches too get up to support him".

Claiming that the wholesale price index (WPI) had risen suddenly after the NF Government assumed power, he asked them how long would they go on blaming the Congress-I for all the ills of the economy.

He said prices of individual items like groundnut oil, *bajra*, *arhar*, and other pulses had risen very sharply in the past few months and compared the decade of price control under the Congress-I regime with the runaway inflation during the short period of NF rule, despite the fact that factors were favourable to it like three good monsoons in a row.

The reason for the deteriorating economic situation, be said, was owing to the belief of the NF Government in populism instead of policies and programmes and because of soft options chosen by it. The "man-made" inflation caused by these would soon cross double digit figure he warned the Government, and said that if not controlled, it would even go up to 20 per cent by the end of the year.

He criticised the measures to control petroleum consumption and castigated the NF Government for the Ministers and their families going all over the world despite the foreign exchange crunch before the country.

*Confederation of Engineering Industry*

The Confederation of Engineering Industry (CEI) has criticised the Government on its economy management and has emphasised the need to avoid *ad hoc* decisions.

In a statement, CEI chief R. Srinivasan said piecemeal and *ad hoc* action is being taken by the Government to meet the developing crisis in regard to foreign exchange resources, import and consumption of petroleum products and generation of additional resources and also conservation. He cited the recent measure relating to this was the 25 per cent increase in prices of petroleum products and 7 per cent increase in corporate tax.

He reiterated the need to set up a joint task force to tackle the current and future economic situation and to adopt a united, Government-industry approach to ensure effective action. The comprehensive action plan should include creation of a nodal agency to work with industry in framing and implementing a total energy conservation programme, reduction in Government expenditure, creation of a climate for foreign investment, and freedom to enterprises to generate additional production.

Srinivasan also suggested that the proposal for workers' participation in management must be deferred and export promotion should be encouraged.

He felt that singling out the corporate sector by raising the corporate tax by seven per cent gives a wrong signal.

(*Hindustan Times*, October 20, 1990)

*II. The Excise Refund*

. . . , the case of duty refunds was merely one of confusion arising out of conflicting court judgments. . . . However, the issue has assumed the dimensions of a scandal with charges being levelled by opposition and even ruling party politicians that certain manufacturing companies had been allowed to withdraw "thousands of crores of rupees" as excise refunds and unjustly enrich themselves.

. . . , Finance Minister Madhu Dandavate asserted in Parliament that no malpractices were involved in the affair. . . . "We have nothing to hide," he said adding that it was baseless to allege that the government had allowed revenue amounting to thousands of crores of rupees to be squandered away.

All this did little to dispel the misgivings of the opposition and demands were made for a Parliamentary probe to find out the persons responsible for the "unjust enrichment" of the manufacturers. This demand was rejected by Dandavate. He did, however, order a stay of further payment of refunds, the total quantum of which, in the past three years, is estimated to be less than Rs.1,3000 crore.

The present controversy started with an order issued to all field officers by the Central Board of Excise and Customs (CBEC) on March 21, 1990, followed by a circular on 28 March, permitting them to decide refund claims for excess payment of excise according to the law.

This was in supersession of instructions issued by a member of the CBEC in 1988 to collectors of central excise to reject claims of refund where the assessee had passed on the burden (of excess payments) to the consumers. These instructions, which in turn superseded guidelines set up by the CBEC on August 10, 1981 to decide refund claims, were on the basis of a Bombay High Court ruling of July 6, 1988.

In that case, popularly known as the Roplas' case, the Court observed: "We are of the view that since the petitioners have already recovered from their customers the whole of the duty, they are not entitled to its refund. Their claim for such refund amounts to a fraud on consumers and society. Any indulgence in their favour will amount to helping them to enrich themselves unjustly."

. . . 1988 instructions followed from this case the benefit of refunds is gobbled up by manufacturers who cannot pass it on to consumers — whom they have excess charged. In fact, these consumers often cannot be traced. The Roplas' judgment helped us to make up our mind.

But, the problem arose because there are a number of court judgments which run counter to the Roplas ruling, while there are several others on the lines of the Roplas judgment. . . . Different benches of the same court and different courts have interpreted the same judgments differently and there is no unanimity in the matter of applicability or otherwise of the doctrine of unjust enrichment in cases of refund of moneys/taxes collected by the state illegally. And this is the crux of the whole problem: the point from which all confusion has arisen.

Before the circular of 28 March this year, collectors of central excise were unable to avoid this ticklish problem. On the one hand, they had instructions from the CBEC (on the basis of the Roplas' case) not to pay refunds, and on the other, assessees flaunted court judgments which ruled in favour of payment of refunds. What compounded problems further was that the 1988 instructions of the CBEC were issued without consulting the law ministry — and thus did not have any legal sanction.

Matters moved towards a settlement last year, when the rejected refund claims (after the instructions of 1988) were admitted in appeal by the Central Excise Customs and Gold Control Appellate Tribunal (CEGAT). The tribunal ruled that the departmental officers did not enjoy the discretion to reject claims of refunds authorised by law on grounds which do not find specific mention in the law itself. This power was enjoyed by high courts and the Supreme Court.

Following this observation, the CBEC consulted the law ministry which opined that there was no proviso in the Central Excise Act by which departmental officers could reject claims on the grounds of unjust enrichment. It was on the basis of this opinion of the law ministry that the CBEC issued its circular of 28 March. It is believed that this circular was issued after a meeting of the whole board of CBEC.

However, even as the controversy rages, some sort of consensus seems to be emerging amongst experts that there should not be any universal rule for payment of refunds. It should be on a case to case basis, and given only when the manufacturer undertakes to pass on the benefit of the refunds to the consumers. There are some court judgments to this effect too.

(Kingshuk Nag, *Business India*, September 17-30, 1990)

**General Observations**

*II. Wholesale Price Index*

There was a sharp increase in the all commodities index by 1.49 per cent in the month of July 1990. This increase was mainly due to a rise in the price of primary articles. The price of manufactured products, on the other hand, remained relatively steady.

*(1980-81 = 100)*

| | 7 Jul '90 | 5 Jun '90 | 8 Jul '89 | % change over | |
|---|---|---|---|---|---|
| | | | | month | year |
| All commodities | 177.5 | 174.9 | 163.2 | 1.49 | 8.76 |
| Primary articles | 181.3 | 176.2 | 163.1 | 2.89 | 11.16 |
| Manufactured products | 177.4 | 175.8 | 164.7 | 0.91 | 7.71 |

*Consumer Price Index*

The consumer price index for industrial workers is up for the fifth consecutive month. Though the increase per month is marginal, if the cement trend continues, the year would end up with double digit inflation. The index for urban non-manual workers is following more or less the same trend.

| | May '90 | Apr '90 | May '89 | % change over | |
|---|---|---|---|---|---|
| | | | | month | year |
| Industrial workers (1982 = 100) | 182 | 180 | 169 | 1.1 | 7.7 |
| Urban non-manual workers (1984-85 = 100) | 153 | 151 | 144 | 1.3 | 6.2 |

*Money and Banking (Scheduled Commercial Banks)*

In keeping with government policy, control has been placed on broad money (M3); this means that the increase will be minimal. Bank credit which had shown a declining trend earlier has risen marginally. Food credit had stabilised at around Rs.3,900 crores.

*(Rs. crore)*

| | 13 Jul '90 | 25 Jun '90 | 14 Jul '89 | % change over | |
|---|---|---|---|---|---|
| | | | | month | year |
| Broadmoney (M3) | 2,37,985 * | 2,37,810 † | 2,03,255 †† | 0.07 | 17.09 |
| Aggregate deposits | 1,72,983 | 1,71,628 | 1,47,807 | 0.79 | 17.03 |
| Bank credit | 1,04,606 | 1,03,837 | 89,023 | 0.74 | 17.50 |
| Food credit | 3,933 | 3,917 | 1,579 | 0.41 | 149.08 |
| Credit/Deposit ratio | 60.47 | 60.49 | 60.23 | –0.03 | 0.40 |

* 29 June 1990; † 30 May 1990 †† 30 June 1989

## *Industrial Production and Infrastructure*

There was a sharp increase in the index of industrial production in March 1990. In the month of May, railway freight increased by 8.1 per cent and there was a decline in the production of crude oil and power generation. Steel production, on the other hand, rose by 6.3 per cent in June after declining by 14.2 per cent in May 1990.

| | Latest month | Previous month | Year ago | % change over | |
|---|---|---|---|---|---|
| | | | | month | year |
| Industrial production index (1980-81 = 100) | 255.3(3) | 206.3 | 208.1 | 23.7 | 22.7 |
| Railway freight (million tonnes) | 26.20(5) | 24.24 | 23.75 | 8.1 | 10.3 |
| Crude oil production ('000 tonnes) | 2875(5) | 2934 | 2825 | -2.0 | 1.8 |
| Power generation (mill. units per day) | 705.7(5) | 710.3 | 624 | -0.70 | 13.0 |
| Coal production (lakh tonnes per day) | 4.8(5) | 4.8 | 4.5 | — | 6.6 |
| Steel production ('000 tonnes) | 639(6) | 601 | 615.6 | 6.3 | 3.8 |
| Cement production ('000 tonnes) | 3902(5) | 3720 | 3740 | 4.9 | 4.3 |

Figures in bracket indicate months.

## *Bullion Prices and Stock Market Index*

While the price of gold has been steady at around Rs.3,300, that of silver has increased by over Rs.200 per kg. Chances of prices going up in the near future are remote. The Bombay stock exchange index is up by a hefty 21.5 per cent. The rise has been due to the favourable monsoon the liberalisation measures announced by the government.

| | 28 Jul '90 | 29 Jun '90 | 2 Jul '89 | % change over | |
|---|---|---|---|---|---|
| | | | | month | year |
| Gold (Bombay) | 3,310 | 3,260 | 3,075 | 1.53 | 7.64 |
| Silver (Bombay) | 6,889 | 6,646 | 6,843 | 3.66 | 0.67 |
| BSE Index (1979-80 = 100) | 1033.15 | 850.50 | 792.17 | 21.52 | 30.42 |

(Price of gold in rupees per 10 gm, silver in rupees per kg)

(*Business India*, August 6-19, 1990)

# EDUCATION

## Promises and Precepts

The National Front will accord the greatest importance to raising the level of national investment in education. It will be the endeavour of the National Front Government to raise the investment to the level of six per cent of national income as the Kothari Commission had recommended. The effort will be to achieve this target by the end of 1995.

Universalisation of elementary education will receive the urgent attention of the National Front Government. It will be our endeavour to achieve compulsory universalisation of elementary education for children up to the age of 14 by the end of 1995. All children will be imparted elementary education in their mother-tongue.

Vocational education at secondary stage needs to be restricted on a large to make education employment-oriented. The National Front government will take necessary and early steps to forge interactive linkages between productive establishments outside the schools. Such vocationalisation of education will be linked to self-employment in agriculture and industry thereby enabling the young to earn while they learn.

The National Front believes that the children should have access to the same standard and type of education. The National Front Government will rectify elitist aberrations in the educational system.

It will abolish capitation fee and other distortions in our educational system. The New Education Policy, introduced by the present Government, has failed to serve the purpose and will therefore, be reviewed and revised.

The National Front will endeavour to help bring a new spirit to our campuses of higher education and foster the growth of research and innovative thinking. It will also give a vigorous push to adult education.

The National Front considers education of the minorities, both religious and linguistic, and of women to be a national responsibility and will take vigorous steps to see that the constraints on their educational progress are removed, as early as possible, through planned and concerted action.

## Process of Action

*Committee for the Review of National Policy on Education, 1986*

In pursuance of its election manifesto, the NF Government announced on May 7, 1990, the appointment of a Committee 'to review the National Policy on Education (NPE), 1986'. The reasons that influenced the decision of the Government as given in the government's resolution are as under:

> *One*, the right to work which is proposed to be enshrined in the constitution;
> *two*, the unity and integrity of the nation that are seriously threatened;
> *three*, the improvement of the inner man in India.

The 17-member committee headed by Acharya Ramamurti set up six groups related to the following aspects:

- Access, Equity and Universal Education
- Education and Right to Work
- Quality and Standard
- National Unity
- Resource and Management and
- Rural Education

In the first meeting of the consultative committee after the formation of the Acharya Ramamurti Committee the education policy was reviewed at a meeting of the Parliamentary Committee for the Ministry of Human Resource Development on May 17, 1990.

Prime Minister V.P. Singh who presided the meeting, said that his Government's emphasis would be on providing access to education for the "disadvantaged, socially backward people, including ethnic and other minority groups.

Referring to the National Front manifesto for the 1989 Lok Sabha elections, Shri Singh said that he would like education being put in the perspective of employment and removal of poverty, and he saw education as a minimum need of people and an investment on human resources.

Shri Singh also wanted universalisation of elementary education, and regional languages as media of instruction, particularly imparting education in the mother-tongue.

Pointing out the importance of adult education, Shri Singh called upon all Parliamentarians to give feedback on their experience in respect of implementing the programmes.

The other points which he emphasised included the national efforts needed for mobilisation of resources for education by balanced Centre-State involvement, steps for the implementation of the recommendations of the Gujral Committee for development of Urdu and abolition of capitation fees.

Minister of State for Human Resource Development Chimanbhai Mehta, while addressing the consultative committee, said that all interested groups will be consulted to make the work of the education policy review committee meaningful.

**Public Opinion**

In an editorial entitled 'Educating Millions' the *Hindustan Times*, dated September 4, 1990, evaluated the work of the NF Government in the field of education in these words, "While it is true that a review of the New Education Policy of 1986 was a campaign issue for the National Front which attacked it for its "elitist aberrations", little effort has been made so far by the Government to define concretely what these "aberrations" are and how these could be eliminated. So far the Government's policy formulations have been long on rhetoric and short on substance as these have come more in the nature of a political attack on its predecessor's education policy than a critical appraisal. It is not enough to underline the need for universalisation of elementary education, access to education for the under-privileged and adult education; the question is why these achievable targets have not been reached. A perspective paper has been prepared by the Acharya Ramamurti Review Committee on education which emphasises the role of education in enabling people for work. A time bound programme for vocational education seems to be the main focus of the review committee. The committee also seeks to phase out the 250-odd Navodaya schools, seen by many as an attempt to spread educational elitism in the rural areas.

Entrenched vested interests in our society have largely sabotaged even the modest schemes for universalising education for the poor. And hence there is an imperative need to change the strategies, and reorient our priorities. India had 26.4 crore illiterates of which 57 per cent are women. By the turn of the century, the country will have half of world' illiterates. Under the circumstances, what we really require is to wage a war on illiteracy. But do we have the political will to undertake the task? The constitutional avowal to ensure free and compulsory education to all up to 14 years within 10 years of the commencement of the Constitution has virtually been forgotten. The renewed avowal made in the previous Government's NEP equally underlined the signal failure to fulfil this obligation. Will the Janata Dal Government succeed where others have failed? Mere pledges are not enough. The nation is already witnessing an upheaval on reservation of job for socially and educationally backward castes. It could have been avoided if the millions down below had been provided access to education."

## EQUALITY AND JUSTICE

### Promises and Precepts

The National Front stands for a fair deal for all the people, particularly for marginalised and oppressed groups — the Scheduled Castes, the Scheduled Tribes and other weaker sections, the bonded labour, the marginal farmers and the artisans.

### Process of Action

No tangible results.

## EX-SERVICEMEN

The National Front reaffirms its commitment to the principle of one-rank-one pension" for ex-servicemen. The welfare of ex-servicemen, hitherto the exclusive responsibility of State Governments, will be made a joint concern of Central and State Governments, with effective monitoring. Steps will be taken to provide meaningful post-retirement employment to defence personnel.

### Process of Action

An *ad hoc* increase in pension has been announced.

**Public Opinion**

I. The special Representative of the Statesman on October 19, 1990, described the reaction of the ex-servicemen over 'one time, ad hoc' increase in their pension, in these words, — the fact that ex-servicemen have let off no firecrackers to celebrate the Government's announcement of a "one time, ad hoc" increase in their pensions is indicative of widespread disappointment. the silence of this generally non-vocal section is telling; it talks aloud of the manner in which the hopes they reposed in the National Front are evaporating.

Though they have yet to organise themselves into a vote bloc, the ex-servicemen had thrown much of their weight behind the National Front last November when its election manifesto had promised implementation of the demand for a system of "one rank, one pension". What the Government now has offered is a far cry from that.

In fact, several ex-servicemen are deeply hurt over what they view as an attempt by the Government to "buy them out". When an official spokesman claimed that the enhanced pensions "approximated" to what the ex-servicemen would have gained if their original demand had been conceded, it became clear that the move had been aimed at meeting the immediate situation.

It is true that many of those neglected old soldiers might accept something as being better than nothing. True also that the discipline instilled into them during their proud period of Colour Service prevents many of them from taking to the streets in protest. But by virtually going back on its word, the National Front has come close to losing its credibility with all those who have worn the uniform, or wear it now.

Even the most handsome and generous offer on a "one time, ad hoc" basis would come nowhere near matching the "one rank, one pension" system. For it is based on a principle — that those who gave of their youth to the nation should spend their later years in the dignity of financial security. that system would end, for all time to come, the discrepancies that have arisen over the years.

Pensions generally are calculated on the basis of the last pay substantially over the years, conditions have been created in which a JCO who retired several years ago actually gets less pension today than someone infinitely less senior who has retired more recently. While this is true of all pensioners — it must be remembered that Servicemen retire in circumstances vastly different from those for civilians.

However, what have not been implemented are the vital ones. And this is what hurts ex-servicemen. There are a few of them in Parliament. Cutting across party affiliations, they have been pressing the demand — but they simply lack the political firepower to force the Government to act.

Some months ago hopes had been generated that another major demand, also recommended by the High-Powered Committee, would be partially met — that of guaranteed employment in other branches of Government until the age of 58. The Prime Minister, with customary fanfare, had spoken of the raising of the National Rifles, in which ex-Servicemen would be drafted to perform specific duties behind the battle zone. The Rifles remain no more than a proposal.

A just deal to ex-servicemen goes beyond repaying the debt owed to those who suffered hardship and risked their lives for the nation. It affects the morale of those in service today — a few years hence they too will qualify for the "ex" prefix. Perhaps most important of all, say ex-servicemen, it influences the decision of the youth considering to opt for the uniform as a way of life."

(*Statesman*, October 19, 1990)

II. The fact that ex-servicemen have let off no firecrackers to celebrate the Government's announcement of a "one time, *ad hoc*" increase in their pensions is indicative of widespread disappointment. The silence of this generally non-vocal section is telling; it talks aloud of the manner in which the hopes they reposed in the National Front are evaporating.

Though they have yet to organize themselves into a vote bloc, the ex-servicemen had thrown much of their weight behind the National Front last November when its election manifesto had promised implementation of the demand for a system of "one rank, one pension". What the Government now has offered is a far cry from that.

In fact, several ex-servicemen are deeply hurt over what they view as an attempt by the Government to "buy them out". When an official spokesman claimed that the enhanced pensions "approximated" to what the ex-servicemen, would have gained if their original demand had been conceded, it became clear that the move had been aimed at meeting the immediate situation.

It is true that many of those neglected old soldiers might accept something as being better than nothing. True also that the discipline installed into them during their proud period of Colour Service prevents many of them from taking to the streets in protest. But by virtually going back on its word, the National Front has come close to losing its credibility with all those who have worn the uniform, or wear it now.

Even the most handsome and generous offer on a "one time, ad hoc" basis would come nowhere near matching the "one rank, one pension" system. For it is based on a principle — that those who gave of their youth to the nation should spend their later years in the dignity of financial security. That system would end, for all time to come, the discrepancies that have arisen over the years.

Pensions generally are calculated on the basis of the last pay drawn. Since pay scales have risen substantially over the years, conditions have been created in which a JCO who retired several years ago actually gets less pension today than someone infinitely less senior who has retired more recently. While this is true of all pensioners — and forms the basis of the bureaucratic blocking of the acceptance of the demand — it must be remembered that servicemen retire in circumstances vastly different from those for civilians.

However, what have not been implemented are the vital ones. And this is what hurts ex-servicemen. There are a few of them in Parliament. Cutting across party affiliations, they have been pressing the demand — but they simply lack the political firepower to force the Government to act.

Some months ago hopes had been generated that another major demand, also recommended by the High-Powered Committee, would be partially met — that of guaranteed employment in other branches of Government until the age of 58. The Prime Minister, with customary fanfare, had spoken of the raising of the National Rifles, in which ex-servicemen would be drafted to perform specific duties behind the battle zone. The Rifles remain no more than a proposal.

A just deal to ex-servicemen goes beyond repaying the debt owed to those who suffered hardship and risked their lives for the nation. It affects the morale of those in service today — a few years hence they too will qualify for the "ex" prefix. Perhaps most important of all, say ex-servicemen, it influences the decision of the youth considering to opt for the uniform as a way of life."

## FERA AND MRTP

### Promises and Precepts

FERA and MRTP Acts shall be strengthened to ensure that

opportunities for expansion are not misused for creating monopolies. Violations of FERA or MRTP shall not be countermanded and provisions of these Acts will be suitably strengthened and strictly enforced.

Ostentatious and elitist consumption, luxurious living, and five-star culture shall be checked by appropriate fiscal policies and other measures.

### Process of Action

No tangible results.

## FISHERMEN

### Promises and Precepts

Non-mechanised fishing will be protected from exploitation by mechanised fishing. Credit facilities and excise duty concessions will be given to small fishermen.

### Process of Action

No tangible results.

## FOREIGN POLICY

*See also*
Nuclear Policy

### Promises and Precepts

*I. Foreign Policy*

The National Front's foreign policy is based on India's traditional values and beliefs, enshrined in the concepts of non-alignment and on the changing realities of the international scene — the world's gradual transition from conflict and confrontation to dialogue, mutual understanding and peaceful cooperation.

India can play its legitimate role in the changing world only by adopting a comprehensive foreign policy which integrates diplomacy, defence economic and cultural policies as well as technological cooperation.

National Front's foreign policy will reject any manipulation from outside. It will strengthen global peace initiatives, the process of nuclear disarmament adopted by USSR, and USA, and will strive for similar limitations to be placed on conventional and chemical weapons. The National Front will pursue the policy of non-alignment and strengthen the non-alignment movement. The NAM will be persuaded to play a more active role in advancement of South-South Cooperation and to diffuse regional tensions. In a spirit of cooperation and mutuality of interests the role of SAARC will be strengthened and furthered. It will also strengthen the positive role of the U.N.

The establishment of New International Economic and Information Orders will be fully supported. It expresses full solidarity with anti-colonial and anti-apartheid struggles, and supports the Palestinians' right of self-determination, the Namibians' struggle for independence, Nicargua's fight against outside interference, the struggle of the Saharwi nationalists and the South African people's struggle against the racist regime.

The National Front government will take bold and creative initiatives to weave a new pattern of cooperative relationship with the neighbours. India's friendship with her traditional friends in South, South-east Asia and West Asia will be further strengthened. The National Front will strive to secure the safety and security of the Tamils in Sri Lanka and promote lasting peace and amity amongst all sections of population in that country. It shall restore our friendly relations with Sri Lanka by withdrawing the Indian Peace Keeping Force.

With Nepal, negotiations will be started on all issues of contention to find an amicable solution. The National Front will help to strengthen the economy of Nepal and honour her self-respect. The National Front will offer to Pakistan mutual withdrawal of VISA restrictions and promotion of bilateral commerce and trade.

The National Front recognises the value of traditional friendship between India and USSR and will strive to further strengthen it while making all efforts to improve friendly relations with USA and other western countries. The National Front believes that normalisation of Sino-Indian relations is in the interests of both countries and will make efforts to improve the expand them without sacrificing national interests.

*II. National Security*

The security of the Nation has been gravely endangered by the Rajiv Gandhi government and made vulnerable to outside pressures. Total absence of a national security doctrine, *ad hoc* decision-making, and easy resort to importing arms, often for extraneous considerations and kickbacks, have all adversely affected the nation's security.

The assessment of external threats to the security of the country should be based on a careful study of the strategic environment. Instead, it has been tailored to the ruling party's immediate needs to gain support for itself. Defence and Diplomacy, which are two sides of the same coin, continue to be pursued in an irrational and arbitrary manner by the present government. Moreover, they are implemented independently of each other, creating confusion all round.

The National Front holds that it is necessary to envolve an overall security doctrine for India, which will be convincingly peace-oriented. The doctrine would take a total view of defence rather than a fractured service by service approach, which is the case at present and would give a central place to self-reliance in defence matters.

Towards this end, the National Front government will establish a NATIONAL SECURITY COUNCIL under the chairmanship of the Prime Minister. The National Security Council will help to evolve a consensus on our foreign and defence policies and coordinate with various Ministries and Departments connected with national security.

**Process of Action**

Intensive dialogue has been initiated for finding mutually acceptable solutions to outstanding problems and enlarging the areas of cooperation.

The traditional ties between India and Nepal, which were under severe strain, have been restored. The Prime Ministers of the two countries signed a Joint Communique to this effect and pledged to work for a new era of cooperation. As a first step the two countries agreed to take administrative and other measures by July 1, 1990 to restore the relationship to the level which existed before April 1987. Simultaneously efforts are being made for arriving at a comprehensive arrangement covering all aspects of bilateral relations.

Our traditional friendly ties with Bhutan and Maldives have been further strengthened. With Bangladesh we have stable relationship.

With the return home of the IPKF from Sri Lanka, we are hopeful that the Sri Lankan Government will fulfil its promises of devolution of power and ensure the safety, security and democratic aspirations of their Tamil-speaking population.

It was India's concern for giving peace a real chance that paved the way for the Simla Agreement. This Agreement has ensured nearly two decades of peace and stability between India and Pakistan. The Government sincerely hopes that Pakistan will honour the Simla Agreement in letter and spirit in the interest of regional peace and stability.

Our relations with the USSR are most stable and our ties with the USA have been improving. There has been a closer dialogue with China to find a fair, reasonable and mutually acceptable settlement of the boundary question.

Our crusade against nuclear weapons continues and we are also continuing our fight for a just world economic order.

India is keen on building up meaningful South-South Cooperation and better dialogue between South and North. The leading role India played at the Group-15 Summit at Kuala Lumpur has set the tone for this cooperation.

## Public Opinion

### *Gulf Crisis*

The former Foreign Secretary, Shri A.P. Venkateshwaran, on October 19, 1990 flayed the Government for not having evolved a "credible foreign policy" to tackle the Gulf crisis.

Participating in a round-table discussion on the Guff crisis organised by the Capital Foundation Society, the former diplomat regretted that "there has been no policy as to what India should say or do to this very day" on the Gulf issue.

Stating that the crisis in the Gulf had to be resolved only by use of force as no opening for peace was visible, Shri Venkateshwaran said under Article 51 of the UN Charter, the United States has got the right to take unilateral action for self-defence.

He termed the situation as "unfortunate". The USSR has effectively disassociated itself from military manoeuvres in the Gulf, as it had to contend itself with domestic changes in recent months, he said.

Shri Venkateshwaran said the role played by the Non-aligned

Movement (NAM) in the Gulf crisis was none too encouraging. Even during the prolonged Iran-Iraq war, NAM didn't contribute much, he said.

He said the recent meeting between India, Yugoslavia and Algeria at Belgrade had turned out to be "a non-starter" from the beginning and put India in an awkward slot for championing its own people's cause.

Shri Venkateshwaran urged the Government to re-examine its foreign policy in the light of successive failures and said the National Security Council (NSC) should initiate certain credible action in this regard.

The Director, Institute of Defence Studies, Shri Jasjit Singh said military option would be very costly for the United States in particular and its allies in general, if a war broke out in the Gulf.

(*Indian Express*, October 20, 1990)

## HEALTH AND FAMILY WELFARE

### Promises and Precepts

It is evident that there has been a serious breakdown in health services in the country. Even the nation's capital has recently witnessed out-break of Cholera and Gastroenteritis epidemics. Preventive, promotive and rehabilitative strategies have failed. Likewise, there has been a serious failure in providing services to the weaker sections specially in remote rural areas.

The National Front will give utmost priority to remedy this sordid state of affairs. Implementation of the Alma Ata Declaration, which assures Health for all by 2000 A.D., will be the major plan or our policy on health and family welfare. Specially it would mean:

(a) Promoting community self-reliance.
(b) Strengthening social control over health services, and
(c) Improving health status by strengthening water supply, environmental, sanitation, nutrition, employment, housing, etc.

While population control will be brought about by a resolute multi-pronged endeavour, the National Front believes that development is the best contraceptive. The present target approach in family planning will be revised to promote and popularise use of contraceptive methods, as well as provide suitable incentives and disincentives. The problem of population growth will be tackled by making various efforts to create conditions where a small family becomes meaningful to the people. The focus will be on reduction in infant mortality, women's education and employment. The National Front will endeavour to bring down the rate of population growth from 2.1 per cent to 1.2 per cent by 2000 A.D.

The National Front will encourage and strengthen indigenous systems of medicine like Ayurveda and Siddha, Unani, Homeopathy and Nature Cure. Research and educational facilities and employment opportunities in these systems of medicines will be promoted.

Occupational health hazard is a serious area of concern. The National Front government will see to it that disasters like the Bhopal gas tragedy are not repeated in future. The rehabilitation of Bhopal gas victims will be treated as a national responsibility.

The drug policy will be revised in line with the recommendations of the Hathi Committee. The reduction in the prices of life-saving drugs and their availability are also part of the National Front's health policy.

**Process of Action**

No tangible results.

## HOUSING AS A RIGHT

**Promises and Precepts**

The National Front will endeavour to develop housing and public transport on a large scale to meet the growing needs of the urban population. The focus of urban development will be shifted from the four metropolises and a score of big cities to thousands of small medium towns. The National Front will introduce a new levy on the urban rich to develop slums into liveable shelters. Environmental considerations will be accorded priority in all urban and rural land-scaping.

Cooperative ownership in urban housing will be promoted on a large scale to ensure shelter for all. Special schemes will be launched to provide the rural poor with adequate housing within the next five years. Developed house sites will also be provided to the poor in urban areas. Foothpath dwellers will be provided shelters.

## Process of Action

### *Draft National Housing Policy*

The Draft National Housing Policy (DNHP) formulated by the National Front Government in the light of its policy thrust and in the contest of the exercise for the formulation of the Eighth Five Year Plan focuses attention on the role of Government and public agencies, investment plan, action plans at State levels among other things.

Releasing the draft policy paper to the Press on June 9, 1990, Minister for Urban Development Murasoli Maran said the thrust of the draft paper is that the Government's crucial role is to create an enabling environment, to remove constraints to housing activity and to promote a substantial increase in the supply of housing and basic services."

He said the Government was aware that housing and urban development policy was primarily implemented by the State and local agencies and hence the housing policy can be finalised only after broadbased consultation with the States and Union territories. Apart from eliciting the views of the States on the draft policy paper, the Centre is also seeking an extensive discussion on the Housing Policy through interaction with experts, specialised bodies, local agencies and voluntary organisations and the general public.

Shri Maran said, in this connection, he has convened regional meetings of experts and others in Madras, Calcutta and Bombay this month and next month. Similar meetings with State Housing Ministers and Chief Executives of housing agencies are also being scheduled, he said.

He said after these interactions, the draft of National Housing policy will be finalised and placed before Parliament. The major issues the policy address include housing norms, supply and management of land, rural housing, slums and squatter settlements, housing finance, building materials and technology, legal and regulatory framework, and investment.

He pointed out that while the backlog of housing needs has persisted and new households have increased with the rise in with rise in population, public investment has steadily declined over successive plan periods. The percentage of housing investment to total investment in the economy has declined from 34 per cent in the First Plan to nine per cent during the Seventh Plan. Government has recognised the immediate need to reverse the declining investment trend in order to tackle the serious dimensions of the housing problem.

The draft paper says that housing norms would be evolved at the regional levels with due regard to different geo-climatic conditions and life styles of the people. The norms and standards would help in promoting the use of local materials and skills as well as the process of incremental construction. It would also seek to prevent the diversion of scarce resources in luxury construction. Minimum as well as maximum housing norms would be prescribed at the national level with allowance for local variations. Appropriate minimum and maximum housing norms in terms of size of plot and dwelling units will be laid down by the State Governments concerned.

The development of house sites and upgradation of housing and rural areas would be linked with activities under the Integrated Rural Development Programme (IRDP) and REEGP investments on the model of Andhra Pradesh.

The paper notes that limitations of the traditional housing finance system could be addressed through a package of programmes which would *inter alia* develop a strengthen and extend housing finance system through provision of support services to spread risks and increase liquidity, develop innovative and non-conventional approaches, operational norms relating to appraisal, sanctions, disbursements and recovery of home loan, develop institutions and delivery mechanisms to provide housing finance services to non-eligible segment of households in rural areas and informal settlements. What is required is the creation of institutional framework that will mobilise savings for housing, meet the credit needs of households and institutions as well as spread risks of home loan originators.

Appropriate changes in the approaches of the existing financial institutions would be made to make them more responsive to the needs of the people. The National Housing Bank would be encouraged to concentrate on the promotion and regulation of housing finance institutions in the public and private sectors, mobilisation of household savings, increasing the access of different income groups to loans, increasing the reach of the poorer sections to housing loans and to concentrate on refinancing operations of financing institutions and cooperatives.

The special role of HUDCO as a techno-financial agency and for expansion of urban infrastructure would be recognised and further expanded. A mortgage insurance scheme under the appropriate enabling legislation would be another step for speedy foreclosure system to enable realisation of defaulted dues by housing finance institutions, the paper says.

The draft paper underlines the need for reorganisation of housing finance system with fiscal measures geared to mobilise savings and resources. Approaches similar to a number of countries of lending at differential rates could be adopted the paper has suggested.

It also suggests creating a secondary mortgage market to attract funds from a broader range of investors and to integrate housing finance with housing market.

As declared by the Union Finance Minister, there is a case for introducing a time bound scheme which would promote the undeclared income and hidden wealth to be used for one or more social purposes such as building houses and slum clearance.

The Government may float bonds, debentures, the proceeds of which may be used entirely for housing the poor provided the source of funds invested in such bond is not questioned. Detailed proposals will be worked out for early introduction of the scheme, the paper says.

The draft paper says appropriate amendments to the existing laws and regulations would be considered for creating an environment for housing activity including amendment to urban land celling act, rent control acts, and other relevant laws.

The paper stresses the importance of reversing the declining investment trend. It is only by stepping up the investment at once in the shelter sector and urban infrastructure and increasing it at a steady pace thereafter there could be significant change in the housing situation. The immediate goal should be to double the investment in public sector during 1990-91 and create conditions for increased flow of funds in the private sector. The share of the financial institutions and Provident Fund should go up to 20 per cent of the annual investment over 1990-95 the paper has suggested.

(*Hindustan Times*, June 10, 1990)

**Public Opinion**

*Housing Policy*

. . . investment in the construction of housing for the people is very welcome indeed. Housing shortage all over the country is the cry of the day. According to the government statistics, the housing needs of the country aggregate during the decade to over 900 lakh dwelling units in rural as well as urban areas, necessitating investment of the order of Rs. 1,40,000 crore excluding the cost of infrastructure and services. If a beginning towards the achievement of this objective can be made with the help of unaccounted money, the nation will heave a sigh of relief because the problem of housing has presently gone completely out of hand. But there are ramifications of this problem which need to be considered in detail. The rent control laws have, besides other inhibiting factors, totally strangulated the construction activity. Nobody now wishes to construct for normal renting. If investment is sought for the housing sector, with the utilisation of unaccounted money, the depredations of rent control laws will need to be obviated in relation to the houses thus constructed.

In sum, what is of paramount importance is the need of encouraging public debate on issues of this nature which at present are featuring in pronouncements and decisions of the present political leadership and causing confusion and unnecessary consternation. It is a matter of deep concern that people are only silently criticising and are not coming forth boldly with the expression of their views. Press and public platforms need to determine what part they have to play in stimulating public debate on such issues.

(*Competition Success Review*, Special Number, 1990)

## IMPORT-EXPORT POLICY

**Promises and Precepts**

The National Front is determined to plug every loophole in the import-export rules and policies which has enabled the anti-social and corrupt elements in industry or government to hoard illegal money in foreign banks. All such money shall be brought back.

**Process of Action**

The Government announced a three-year Import-Export Policy

**Public Opinion**

*Stimulus to Exports*

The *Import-Export Policy (1990-93)* announced recently is designed to encourage rapid and sustained export growth including export services which are becoming important in world commerce. It provides export industry with reasonably easy access to the imported inputs and capital goods.

A notable feature of the Policy is simplification of procedures. For the first time, the Government has finalised and introduced two master documents which will greatly simplify the existing documentation system. 'Common facility documentation centres' are proposed to be established at various places to make it possible for small exporters to prepare the required documents at minimum cost and delay. The shift is towards reposing greater trust in the export community and reducing controls. While continuing the liberal thrust, the Policy has also made a serious attempt to plug loopholes and curtail unnecessary imports to cope with the difficult Balance of Payments position.

While making it clear that public sector has a very important role to play in development, the Government at the same time has signalled that private sector could participate in infrastructure development, including power generation.

## INDUSTRIALISATION

### Promises and Precepts

In the industrial sphere present policies are biased towards large sized, capital-intensive urban-based industries. Even the small-scale industries, which have prospered in recent years, have largely been ancillaries of urban-oriented service industries. Their potential for creation of additional employment has been limited and the commodities they produce meet mainly the requirements of affluent sections. Simultaneously, a large number of small-scale and village industries, which have for centuries provided gainful employment to men and women in all parts of the country, have been woefully neglected. Millions of jobs in these industries have been sacrificed to satisfy the captains of industries in the large-scale private-sector as is evident from the Government's National Textile Policy of 1985, encouragement of harvestor combines and other labour displacing machinery in various sectors. The impact of these policies has been very severe on some of the poorest States like Bihar and Uttar Pradesh.

The National Front Government will promote industrial development in such a way as to maximise employment. The emphasis will be on producing wage goods and services required for consumption by the mass of our people. Agro-processing industries, industries based on the craft of rural artisans, village industries of particular benefit to women and rural households will receive full sport by way of credit, extension service, supply of inputs, marketing organisation, etc. Manufacture of items of mass consumption, which can be produced by the cottage and small-scale industries, will be reserved for these centres.

In respect of infrastructure and capital goods industries we shall modify the conditions and parametres to ensure efficiency in the utilisation of investment and relevance to national priorities in end-use. The commanding position will continue to be occupied by the public sector which will be made more managerially efficient and less dominated by the bureaucracy. Infrastructure development will again be oriented to the better distribution of goods, services and benefits.

The strategy of development pursued so far, and more brazenly in the eighties, has made the country increasingly subservient to foreign capital in order to satisfy the demand pattern of the affluent 10 per cent population. In the name of technological upgradation, the liberalised import of capital goods and trunkey projects has blocked indigenous enterprise for the development of industries on a self-reliant basis, including such vital industries as transport, steel, chemicals, power and engineering. In addition, Indian big business and transnational corporations have been allowed, on an increasing scale, to manufacture all kinds of consumer goods, including foods and toiletery in which the small producers are efficient and viable. The so-called latest and sophisticated technologies have been imported without taking into consideration their impact on employment. Indiscriminate automation and thoughtless computerisation has been resorted to, thereby allocating scarce capital resources for labour displacement and increasing the country's dependence on foreign capital. The impact of this on indigenous R & D and meaningful development of Indian Scientists and Technologists has been most deleterious and utilisation of their talents has been on the decline.

**Process of Action**

*New Industrial Policy*

I. Text of the industrial policy paper presented by Industry Minister

Ajit Singh in Parliament on May 31, 1990.

Government have been considering the need to take measures for promotion of small scale and agro-based industries and to change procedures for grant of industrial approvals.

In pursuance of our policy to reorient industrial growth to serve the objective of employment generation, dispersal of industry in the rural areas, and to enhance the contribution of small scale industries to exports it has been decided to take the measures enumerated below:

The investment ceiling in plant and machinery for small scale industries (fixed in 1985) would be raised from the present Rs. 35 lakh to Rs. 60 lakh and correspondingly, for ancillary units from Rs 45 lakh to Rs 75 lakh. In order to enable small scale industries to play an important role in the total export effort, such of the small scale units which undertake to export at least 30 per cent of the annual production by the third year will be permitted to step up their investment in plant and machinery to Rs 75 lakh.

Investment ceiling in respect of tiny unit would also be increased from the present Rs 2 lakh to Rs 5 lakh. However, with regard to their location, the population limit of 50,000 as per 1981 Census would continue to apply. Steps will be taken to ensure better inflow of credit and other vital inputs and to improve the infrastructural support to the constituents of the tiny sector.

Presently, 836 items have been reserved for exclusive manufacture in the small scale sector. Efforts would be made to identify more items amenable to similar reservation. Encroachment and violation by large scale units into areas reserved for small scale sector will be effectively dealt with.

A new Scheme of Central Investment Subsidy exclusively for the small scale sector in rural and backward areas capable of generating higher level of employment of lower capital cost would be implemented.

With a view to improving the competitiveness of the products manufactured in the small scale sector, programmes for modernisation and upgradation of technology would be implemented. A number of technology centres, tool rooms, process and product development centres, testing centres, etc., will be set up under the umbrella of an apex technology development centre in Small Industries Development Organisation.

To ensure adequate and timely flow of credit for the small scale industries, a new apex bank known as SIDBI has already been established. One of the major tasks of SIDBI and other commercial banks/financial institutions would be to channellise need-based, higher flow of credit, both by way of term loan and working capital, to the tiny and rural industries. A targeted approach will be adopted to ensure implementation and to facilitate monitoring this objective.

The existing regime of fiscal concessions will be reviewed both to provide sustained support to the units in the small scale sector and to remove the disincentives for their graduation and further growth.

An exercise will be undertaken to identify locations in rural areas endowed with adequate power supply and intensive campaigns will be launched to attract suitable entrepreneurs, provide all other inputs and foster small scale and tiny industries. Similarly, industries which are not energy-intensive will be identified for proliferation in rural areas where power supply is presently a constraint.

In order to widen the entrepreneurial base, the Government would lay particular emphasis on training of women and youth under the Entrepreneurial Development Programme. A special cell would be established in SIDO and State Directorates of Industries to assist women entrepreneurs.

One of the persistent complaints of the small scale units is their being subjected to a large number of acts/laws, being required to maintain a number of registers, submit plethora of returns and face an army of inspectors, particularly in the field of labour legislations. These bureaucratic controls will be reduced so that unnecessary interference is eliminated. Further, procedure will be simplified and paper work cut down.

In order to assist the large number of artisans engaged in the rural and cottage industries, the activities of the KVIC and KVI boards will be expanded, and these organisations, will be strengthened to discharge the responsibility more effectively. Special marketing organisations at the Centre and State levels shall be created to assist rural artisans in marketing their products and also in supply of raw materials. Besides, providing concessional credit, training facilities and free consultancy to groups of artisans will also be provided.

In agro-processing industries industries greater success has been achieved where growers and processors have been integrated, as in the case of sugar. For the success of other agro-based industries also, close links must be forged between the growers and processor units. Industrial Policy will therefore, especially promote projects which are organised in close cooperation on the basis of joint ownership.

Growers will be encouraged to set up processing units within the framework of cooperative societies or similar institutional framework. This will also ensure the transmission of better technology for enhanced agricultural production.

In sectors where units require licensing, the policy will also encourage location of processing units in rural areas where growers are concentrated. Apart from economic benefits of proximity to raw materials it will help in dispersal of industry and increasing employment in rural areas.

Agro-processing industry will receive high priority in credit allocation from the financial institutions. In apportionment of working capital, banks will give high priority to such industries as compared to the rest of the industrial sector.

In order to bring the best technology available to these industries, technology approvals will be given within 30 days of presentation to the Secretariat for Industrial Approvals in the Department of Industrial Development. Government will actively promote the generation, adaptation and adoption of new technologies in the field.

*Procedures for Industrial Approvals*: Indian industry must be made more competitive internationally. It also needs to be released from unnecessary bureaucratic shackles by reducing the number of clearances required from the Government. While the Government will continue to examine large projects in view of resource constraints, decisions in respect of medium sized investments will be left to the entrepreneurs. To achieve these objectives, the following decisions have been taken.

*Delicensing*: All new units up to an investment of Rs 25 crore in fixed assets in non-backward areas and Rs 75 crore in Centrally-notified backward areas will be exempt from requirement of obtaining licence/registration.

*Capital Goods*: For the import of capital goods, the entrepreneur would have entitlement to import up to a landed value of 30 per cent of the total value of plant and machinery required for the unit.

*Raw Materials and Components*: For imports of raw materials and components, imports will be permissible up to a landed value of 30 per cent of the ex-factory value of annual production. The ex-factory value of production will exclude the excise duty on the item of production. Raw materials and components of OGL will not be included within this 30 per cent limit. For all licensable items of raw materials and components, import licensing procedures will continue to operate.

*Foreign Collaboration*: In respect of transfer of technology, if import of technology is considered necessary by the entrepreneur, he can conclude an agreement with the collaborator, without obtaining any clearance from the Government, provided that royalty payment does not exceed 5 per cent on domestic sales and 8 per cent on exports. If, however, lump sum payment is involved in the import of technology, the proposal will require technology, the proposal will require Government clearance, but a decision will be communicated to the entrepreneur within a period of 30 days.

*Foreign Investment*: Keeping in view the need to attract effective inlow of technology, investment up to 40 per cent of equity will be allowed on an automatic basis. In such proposals also, the landed value of imported C.G. shall not exceed 30 per cent of value of plant and machinery.

*Minimum Economic Size*: In order to ensure that investment leads to production of goods that attain international competitiveness and that maximum efficiency is ensured, the unit would have to conform to the minimum economic size in cases where such a size has been prescribed.

*Expansion*: The de-regulation suggested above would cover all cases of expansion and would not be restricted only to new units.

*Broadbanding*: The existing broadbanding scheme would continue to be in force. In addition, if no extra investment is required, no clearance from the Government would be necessary for production and sale of any new item by existing units. This would not include those items which are reserved for small scale industries.

*Location Policy and Environmental Clearances*: The location policy would not be applied to such industries by the Centre except for location in and around metropolitan cities with population above four million. For these cities location will not be permissible within 20 km calculated from the periphery of the metropolitan area except in prior designated industrial areas and for non-polluting industries such as electronics, computer software and printing. It will be up to State Governments to regulate industrial locations keeping in mind local conditions and requirements and their respective spatial development plans, and zoning and town planning laws. Similarly, environmental clearance would have to be obtained from the prescribed authority at the State level. In future should Central legislation introduce new provisions, that law would automatically apply to these units as well.

*Export Oriented Units*: Hundred per cent export oriented units

(EOUs) and units to be set up in export processing zones (EPZs) are also being delicensed under the scheme up to an investment limit of Rs 75 crore.

*Convertibility Clause*: Such investments shall be exempt from the "Convertibility Clause" applicable to financing by Indian Financial Institutions.

It may be clarified that in the application of the proposals listed above, 836 items which are reserved for production in the small scale sector will continue to be excluded.

The above proposals will be applicable to all manufacturing items in a specified list. The list shall follow the nomenclature of the Indian trade classification based on the harmonised systems. In each section of the classification, apart from positive mention of approved items, those not permissible shall be specifically excluded from the benefit of the proposals listed above. Approval for excluded items will be as per the existing industrial policy regime and procedures.

Units set up by MRTP/FERA companies will be covered by the procedures set out above, but they will continue to need clearances under the provisions and regulations of these two Acts.

*The Existing De-licensed Industries Scheme*. Exempted Industries Scheme and DGTD Registration System will stand abolished.

II. Extracts from an interview with the Minister and published in *Business India* in June 11-24, 1990 a day after the Industrial Policy was announced:–

*General Objectives of the Policy*: The policy is essentially a set of measures designed to begin a process of change in Indian industry which would enable all segments in the industrial sector to grow in the nineties. An exercise of this kind can never be comprehensive and complete. The present policy is basically aimed at the small scale sector and subsequent instalments of the policy will be targeted at MRTP companies.

We have already started the process of economic liberalisation. The industrial policy just announced is only the first phase. The next will open up the economy further. It is being worked out now. All I can say is that the large sector will also be affected.

As a result of this policy, we expect to effectively free the majority of industrial investments from delays which are endemic in a bureaucratic clearance system. Under the new scheme of things 60-65 per cent of all intended investments will not require any clearance from the central government. I am saying this on the basis of an analysis of different kinds of industrial approvals required. I want to do away with the committees of ministers and secretaries and all that.

The remaining 30-35 per cent would continue to require the appropriate approvals, but we will ensure that these are dealt within a period of 30 days. If required, we will have a legislative provision.

*Foreign Investment Policy*: We are contemplating a change in the present foreign investment policy. There will be no hike in the 40 per cent equity ceiling on foreign shareholding. But all other aspects of the foreign investment policy are being examined. A negative list of industries is also being drawn up where foreign investment will not be allowed.

We do hope that foreign investors are satisfied with the new policy, because their main complaint concerns the elaborate procedures in this country. This policy will lead to an increase in inflow of foreign investment.

The clause in the new policy enabling firms to induct foreign technology without referring to the government will not bring in repetitive technology as is believed by some. The idea is to enhance the process of technological upgradation. It does not matter if this leads to indigenous technology being ignored, as the country requires the best technology possible.

Foreign investment and technological collaboration will curb domestic competition. They will have to pull up their socks and quality will have to be the hallmark. Let our industries be able to survive in the international market.

*Policy Towards Small-scale and Agro-based Industry*: This policy is also designed to raise exports. The limits for small-scale industries have been raised so that they can become more competitive and export more. We are also thinking of raising the excise concession limit, so that units which will be small scale as a result of the raised investment limit in the new policy can also take advantage of this. The matter has been taken up with the finance ministry.

An enlargement of the list of items reserved for the small-scale sector is being contemplated. An exercise is on at Udyog Bhavan for framing new guidelines for growth centres. An enhancement in the limit for the small-scale sector will not induce large houses to set up subsidiary units in the small scale, as many think it will. Any way, it does not matter, because we are interested in production.

Agro-processing units will also get an impetus as a result of the new policy. The newly set up bank for small-scale industries has been given instructions to give priority to agro-processing units in the matter of giving loans. We have definitely decided to make our economy agriculture-based. We will also welcome foreign technology in the agro-processing sector. Though some people might call this exploitation, I do not see anything wrong in this. In fact this is giving the farmer his due, by enabling higher return for his produce.

*Achievements of V. P. Singh's Government*: Have you seen our manifesto? Employment was one of the major priorities. The new industrial policy is aimed at generating more work, hence the impetus to small-scale industries. Within the inherited constraints, we have already changed the direction of the economy by easing bureaucratic controls.

*III. Highlights of New Industrial Policy (May 1990)*

* All new units up to an investment of Rs 25 crores in fixed assets in non-backward areas and Rs 75 crores in Centrally-notified backward areas will be exempt from licensing/registration.
* 100 per cent export-oriented units and new units in export processing zones delicensed up to the investment limit of Rs 75 crores.
* Under the broadbanding scheme existing units will not have to obtain clearance from the Government for producing and selling new items if no extra investment is made.
* The location policy for such industries has been relaxed.
* Raw materials and components up to 30 per cent of the landed value of the ex-factory value of annual production to be permitted. Capital goods import up to the landed value of 30 per cent of total value of plant and machinery allowed.
* No prior clearance needed for foreign collaboration if royalty payment does not exceed certain limits. Foreign investment up to 40 per cent of the equity will be allowed on an automatic basis.
* Investment ceiling in plant and machinery for small scale industries raised to Rs 60 lakhs and for ancillary units to Rs 75 lakhs.
* Investment ceiling for tiny units raised to Rs 5 lakhs.
* To ensure that investment leads to production of goods acceptable internationally, units will have to conform to minimum economies of size.

* High priority to be given to agro-based industries. Special marketing agencies for the products of rural and cottage industries to be set up by the Centre and the States.
* Special emphasis on training women entrepreneurs. Youth also to be trained to set up industries.

The New Industrial Policy (May 1980) provides for

— Greater promotion of small scale and agro-based industries and simplifying of procedures for industrial approvals.
— Investment ceiling in plant and machinery for small scale industries raised from the present Rs 35 lakh to Rs 60 lakh and for ancillary units from Rs 45 lakh to Rs 75 lakh.
— A new Central investment Subsidy Scheme for small scale sector in rural/backward areas capable of generating more jobs at lower capital costs.
— High priority to agro-processing industry in credit allocation from financial institutions.
— Emphasis on training of women and youth under the Entrepreneurial Development Programme.
— Expansion of activities of the KVIC and KVI Boards.
— Creation of special marketing organisations at the Centre and States to assist rural artisans in marketing their products and also in supply of raw materials, concessional credit, training facilities and free consultancy.

*See also*
Licensing Policy

**Public Opinion**

*WUPCCI*

Western UP Chamber of Commerce and Industry (WUPCCI) president Mahendra K. Modi congratulated the National Front Government for taking bold steps in removing procedural/bureaucratic delays which would go a long way in the rapid industrial development of the country and more particularly in creating a more conducive climate.

In a statement, Shri Modi welcomed the new industrial and foreign investment policy and supported the increase in the investment limits for small-scale units from Rs 35 lakh to Rs 60 lakhs (Rs 75 lakh for the exporting units), for ancillary units from Rs 45 lakh to Rs 75 lakh and for medium scale units from Rs 5 crore to Rs 25 crore.

He felt that the spirit behind the liberalisation would result in faster industrialisation and hoped that Indian industry would become more competitive internationally as there would be a free inflow of imported technology, capital goods and raw materials/components etc.

Considering this approach, the industry expects similar liberalisation and elimination of procedural hold ups for MRTP and FERA companies so that the country may continue to march ahead in industrialisation, Shri Modi added.

*CEI*

The Confederation of Engineering Industry (CEI) has welcomed the new policy and has praised Industry Minister Shri Ajit Singh for his initiative in simplifying and smoothening the procedural hassles.

In a statement in Delhi CEI president V. Srinivasan has expressed satisfaction that a number of recommendations of the CEI have been accepted by the Government. He said the liberalised norms of foreign collaborations, delicensing of medium-sized investment, easier norms for import of capital goods, raw materials and components, extension of minimum economic size, raising of investment limit for small-scale industry and ancillary units would boost industrial growth considerably.

The CEI president hoped that its recommendation with regard to increasing the threshold limit of FERA/MRTP companies, opening of Appendix *I*, revision of Schedule A, opening of defence, mining, power and telecom sectors to private enterprise, would be considered in the next round of policy announcements.

*IEEMA*

The Indian Electrical and Electronics Manufacturers' Association (IEEMA) president Vinay Rai has also hailed the new policy as pragmatic approach for stimulating growth . . . in a new revolution in the country, . . . small and medium scale industries would have wider and constructive role to play. FEII president B. D. Aggarwal and vice-president I. P. Jain have specially praised the Industry Minister for his "innovative ideas to raise the investment limits of the small-scale as well as ancillary units".

*BCC*

Commenting on the new industrial policy announced, president of the Bharat Chamber of Commerce (BCC), J. Khemani said that the National Front Government deserved appreciation for formulating the new industrial policy which contained many laudable features. The implementation of the new policy would go a long way in achieving the cherished objectives of the decentralised industrial growth, generation of more employment opportunities and eradication of poverty.

The Industry Minister was to be congratulated particularly for raising in the investment ceiling on plant and machinery for small-scale industries from Rs 35 lakh to Rs 60 lakh, for ancillary units from Rs 45 lakh to Rs 70 lakh, and for tiny units for Rs 2 lakh to Rs 5 lakh, delicensing of new units up to a limit of Rs 25 crore in fixed assets in non-backward areas and Rs 75 crore in backward areas, liberalised normal for foreign collaboration and for saving the small-scale units from being subjected to numerous acts and laws and submission of a plethora of returns, simplification of procedures and cutting down of paper work.

*ICC*

President of the Indian Chamber of Commerce (ICC), Sanjiv Goenka has complimented the Industry Minister for giving a greater thrust and freedom to small and medium scale industries.

Delicensing of new units, liberalised norms for foreign collaboration, freedom to import capital goods and exemption of such investments from convertibility clause were steps in the right direction. These liberalisations would reduce delays and attain greater dispersal of industries.

Shri Goenka, however, said that nothing had been done for the MRTP and FERA companies. He felt that considering the bold steps the Industry Minister had taken for the small and medium industries, he could have given greater freedom to MRTP and FERA companies.

*IMC*

The Indian Merchants' Chamber (IMC) has welcomed the new industrial policy announced and said it was a further step towards crystallising the liberalisation policy initiated since 1985.

Chamber President M. K. Sanghi, said the most relieving feature was the open ended approach to foreign investment up to 40 per cent equity particularly problem of industrial sickness and gross inefficiencies in public sector management. Attention to these two issues would help conserve a major part of investible resources currently locked up or going waste, he added.

*MCCI*

Maharashtra Chamber of Commerce and Industries (MCCI) here has welcomed the new industrial policy.

The policy has fulfilled the need for more liberal delicensing and deregulation necessary to make our industry internationally competitive, an MCCI Press release issued here said.

The chamber welcomed the raising of investment ceiling in plant and machinery for small-scale industries to Rs 60 lakh from the present Rs 35 lakh.

The raising of delicensing limits to Rs 25 crore in respect of new units in non-backward areas and Rs 75 crore in backward areas will no doubt, considerably cut down the gestation period, the release said. Additional procedural reliefs given in respect of export promotion, technology transfer, foreign investment, strengthening of infrastructure should create a new hope, the release added.

*SICCI*

The Southern India Chamber of Commerce and Industry (SICCI) has said the new industrial policy would 'greatly help' accelerate industrial development and promote exports.

Welcoming the raising of the investment limit for the small sector to Rs 60 lakh, SICCI president M. A. Alagappan in a statement here said the import entitlement for capital goods as well as the incentives for import of raw material would help to enhance India's competitive capacity in foreign markets and increase production of quality goods.

The new facility to conclude agreements with foreign collaborators without obtaining clearance, subject to limitations, would greatly help import the best technology. The policy would also encourage more foreign investment since equity up to 40 per cent would be allowed on automatic basis.

Shri Alagappan said the clause providing for conversion of loan into equity could, however, be suitably modified to encourage share prices.

*HCC*

President of the Hindustan Chamber of Commerce (HCC), Vummidi Nandagopal, has welcomed several features of the new policy.

Describing it as a 'growth-oriented policy', Shri Nandagopal said in a statement that the raising of investment ceiling in plant and machinery for small-scale industries from Rs 35 lakh to Rs 60 lakh and that of ancillary units from Rs 45 lakh to Rs 75 lakh, was in view of inflation.

The proposed scheme of Central investment subsidy exclusively for the small-scale sector in rural and backward areas capable of generating higher levels of employment at lower capital costs would encourage entrepreneurs to set up industries in those areas and reduce the unemployment problem to a large extent, he said.

*BNCCI*

The Bengal National Chamber of Commerce and Industry (BNCCI), today welcomed the new industrial policy, saying that it had several positive features.

In a Press release here, BNCCI president A. K. Chandra, said that raising the investment ceiling in plant and machinery for small-scale and ancillary industries, delicensing of new units up to an investment of Rs 25 crore in non-backward areas and Rs 75 crore in backward areas, liberalising norms for foreign collaboration and automatic clearance up to 40 per cent of equity would help in small and ancillary industries.

While appreciating the Government's intention to reduce bureaucrative controls on the small-scale sector, he regretted that it had not declared specific steps to reduce formalities, particularly regarding labour legislation.

Mr Chandra, however, felt that the Government's policy of allowing investment up to Rs 75 lakh in plant and machinery for small-scale units, exporting at least 30 per cent of their annual production was "not realistic".

(*Hindustan Times*, June 4, 1990)

*PHDCCI — Experts*

The senior industrialists and economists, at a meeting convened by Shri R. K. Somany, President of PHD Chamber of Commerce and Industry to discuss the new industrial policy document on June 10, 1990 observed that the new industrial policy was in tune with the priorities and objectives of the National Front Government and now is the need for proper infrastructure planning, because without adequate infrastructure facilities there may be growth of industrial units all over the country but there will be tremendous increase in industrial sickness.

The experts, said Shri Somany, felt that following increase in the investment limit for tiny, ancillary and small scale units, there is going to be an unprecedented growth in manufacturing activities all over the country.

At present there are about two million registered small scale units and if we consider only the registered units it comes to about two units for every 200 families. However, in the near future, the experts were of the view, it would be about four units for every 200 families.

It is in this context that Shri Somany felt the present policy with regard to the small scale sector, tiny and ancillary sectors will resolve the problem of unemployment by the end of the decade. At the same time, he pointed out that very soon the country may face acute shortage of skilled and semi-skilled workers unless proper manpower planning for industrial growth is initiated urgently.

Further, this would exert tremendous pressure on the existing infrastructure and basic raw materials like iron and steel, coal power, etc.

## INSTITUTIONAL FINANCE

### Promises and Precepts

The public financial institutions shall be required to reorient their investment and credit policies in favour of the poor and down-trodden groups such as cultivators and artisans, agro-industries and small and medium sector industries.

Suitable mechanism through financial institutions will be worked out to enable workers acquire shares in industrial enterprises in which they are employed.

**Process of Action**

No tangible results.

## INVESTMENT ON THE PEOPLE

**Promises and Precepts**

The National Front's policy of socio-economic development will centre round the people, their right to productive and gainful work and eradication of mass poverty. Priority will be given to direct investment on the people, that is, on the provision of basic needs: education, nutrition, health, drinking water, housing, sanitation and easy access to items of essential consumption at subsidised prices. These will enable the people to make their full contribution to advancement of our socio-economic, political and cultural life.

**Process of Action**

No tangible results.

## JUDICIARY

**Promises and Precepts**

*Independence of Judiciary*

Nothing has hurt the rule of law and the provision of a just and humane framework of governance as the present government's attempt to compromise an independent judiciary. The National Front Government will take steps to restore the independence of the judiciary.

Steps will be taken to speed the process of law. The powers of the Executive to influence the appointments and transfers of judges will be eliminated. A high-level judicial commission will be entrusted with these powers. The number of judges will be constantly reviewed, and *ad hoc* appointments will also be sanctioned to clear the huge backlog of pending cases expeditiously. The system of Nyaya Panchayats and Lok Adalats in settling cases by mutual discussion will be strengthened and extended. Free legal aid to the poor will be made a reality.

**Process of Action**

A judiciary that is not only independent but is also perceived to be independent is essential to the healthy functioning of our democracy. This is proposed to be ensured by setting up a high-level Judicial Commission under the Constitution for the appointment of High Court and Supreme Court Judges and the transfer of High Court Judges. A Bill to this effect has been introduced in Parliament.

Constitution (67th) Amendment Bill relating to National Judicial Commission introduced.

**Public Opinion**

*National Judicial Commission*

. . . the National Front Government has introduced the Constitution (67th) Amendment Bill. . . . The Bill deals with the appointment of a National Judicial Commission which would deal with the appointment of the Supreme Court and High Court judges. Also the modality for the appointment of High Court judges is provided.

The Bill sought to vest the power of selecting Supreme Court judges in a panel of three judges headed by the Chief Justice of India. The Government has now taken note of the fact that this would dilute the authority of the Chief Justice of India. The two judges may not agree with the Chief Justice. One can only hope that the Government would consider the matter deeply before arriving at a decision in the appointment of judges, the Chief Justice's view should certainly carry weight but his must not be the only voice. No person, howsoever high, is free from prejudice or foibles. If two senior colleagues differ with him, it only would show that there is something wrong with the Chief Justice's choice.

Two facts have exercised the public mind over the higher judiciary increasing corruption and appointments on considerations other than merit, the constitutional provision of consultations with the Chief Justice of India and the High Court Chief Justices (where High Court appointments are concerned) having been reduced to a farce, by the Rajiv Gandhi and Mrs. Gandhi Governments.

Thus the higher judiciary has been facing threats both from within and without. And the question is what can be done about it. . . .

The Chief Justice of India, Shri Sabyasachi Mukharji some weeks before his death did well to take the nation into confidence and tell it first in advance what the Chief Justices' Conference intended to discuss and later let it know what the decisions were.

What the Chief Justices had now decided was that the Chief Justice of India and the Chief Justices of High Courts had the power to receive complaints against Judges — a fact that was never clear before and, in any case had not been exercised until Shri Justice Ramaswamy was asked by Chief Justice Mukharji to proceed on leave.

When a High Court Chief Justice receives a complaint he would look into it in order to find out if it deserves a closer scrutiny. If it does, he shall have the facts ascertained in such manner as he considers appropriate, keeping the nature of allegations in view.

If he is satisfied that the matter deserves to be reported to the Chief Justice of India, he would do so.

The Chief Justice of India shall follow the same procedure except that he will himself have to decide what to do with a judge against whom adverse facts have been found. While briefing journalists, the Chief Justice added, "On the basis of the facts ascertained, the Chief Justice of the High Court or the Supreme Court, as the case may be, will take such appropriate action as may be considered proper keeping the interests of the judiciary as paramount consideration."

This would imply that there could be an intermediate stage, as far as the High Court Chief Justice is concerned, between reporting the matter to the Chief Justice of India and dropping the matter. Could the High Court Chief Justice ask a judge against who an allegation has been made to go on leave or stop giving him assignments on his own? But the more significant observation by Chief Justice Mukharji was: "in view of the fact that the complaints against the judges would be looked into a manner above, there would be no scope for grievance on this score."

"Therefore, the Bar or the media would have no justification publicly to discuss such conduct and in the event to such public degeneration of judges, it would be open to action under the appropriate law. All who have no cause to despair in view of the above procedure".

In plain terms, the Chief Justice of India wants all public criticism of judges to stop. He wants complains against judges to be treated on par with complaints against Ministers, as contemplated in the Lok Pal Bill; no public hearing, no publication of the matter being investigated, no detailed public knowledge of the evidence which has gone in favour of or against the judge complained against. In a way the procedure contemplated by the Chief Justice is a little worse. At least, the conduct of the Minister against whom there has been a complaint of corruption will be investigated by the Lok Pal (three Supreme Court Judges) and not the Prime Minister but in the case of judges the matter will be exclusively handled either by the High Court Chief Justice or the Chief Justice of India. It has not even been suggested that senior colleagues would necessarily be consulted by either Chief Justice. They may or may not be. In the present cynical mood of the Nation (for good reasons), it would not wholly trust a single individual, howsoever highly placed. Quirks on the part of the Chief Justices cannot be entirely ruled out.

As for publication of reports and criticism in the media, one must wholly condemn the recent excesses by the Press or the Bar but every publication of fact does not constitute a degeneration of a judge or the judiciary. Veiled threat of action under the Contempt of Courts Act needs to be noted. While one would not defend reckless criticism of judges, one needs to emphasise that much will depend on how the judges conduct themselves. The malady seems to have gone deep into the system. One former Chief Justice of India thought as many as 80 High Court Judges needed to be transferred. Contempt powers are a poor shield for the judiciary and can be reached by collective defiance, Surely to court can put the entire bar or the media personnel behind bars.

One must hasten to add that, at the same time, the bar and the media cannot arrogate themselves, the power to decide who is corrupt and who is not, who among the judges deserves to be in office or enjoy public confidence. It is in the interests of the nation that the judiciary should be held in high esteem. This would be possible only if both the judges and the media play their respective roles, within their own bounds. Even former Chief Justices now concede that the Contempt of Courts Act needs to be amended to as to make truth defence. Equally no newspaper or the editor has a right to declare a judge unfit to sit on the Bench. Comments such as this expose the lack of maturity of a journalist.

Chief Justice Mukharji also let it be known that the Chief Justices thought that there was nothing particularly wrong in the present mode of appointment and transfer of judges, except that they wanted the appointments to be made with the concurrence of the Chief Justice of India. Confessedly, the Chief Justices now want Parliament to undo what the Supreme Court itself has done to deny a place of privacy to the Chief Justice of India in appointments and transfers and to hand over to the Government the overriding power in matters of appointments. Thus, indirectly, the Chief Justices cannot be allowed to have the last word on the subject.

In an article written for a national daily, a former Chief Justice of Andhra Pradesh High Court has suggested that the best way to deal with corruption among judges would be suitably to amend the provisions of the Judges Inquiry Act so that the Chief Justice of India is able to refer to a committee appointed by the Speaker of the Lok Sabha and comprising a judge of the Supreme Court, a Chief Justice of a High Court and distinguished jurist to inquire into allegations to corruption against judge. Under the Act such an inquiry is possible after a petition by MPs in the prescribed manner to the President.

The Act is part of the proceedings to impeach a judge and what the former Andhra Pradesh Chief Justice has in mind is a procedure simpler than impeachment but which would keep the primacy of the Chief Justice of India intact. The proposal merits serious consideration.

(*Competition Success Review*, November 1990)

## LABOUR

### Promises and Precepts

#### *1. Labour Policy*

The workers in factories will be made effective partners in management at plant and shop levels so that their willing cooperation in increasing production can be secured and conditions of industrial peace and democracy can be promoted. The repressive and obnoxious features of the industrial relations law will be replaced by more democratic and rational provisions. Article 311 of the Constitution will be restored to its original position to ensure security against arbitrary dismissal of government servants. Recognition of trade unions on the basis of workers' support will be determined by secret ballot.

The National Front promises regularisation of casual labour in various government departments and public undertakings, having regard to the length of their continuous service. Delays, arbitrariness and circumventions shall not be allowed to hamper conciliation and arbitration in collective bargaining. The Indian Labour Conference will be activated to help create harmonious industrial relations and increase productivity.

For the workers in the unorganised sectors of the economy, including construction workers, appropriate legislation will be undertaken to ensure security against arbitrary removal, provision of fair wages, maternity benefits, safety and adequate accident compensation, creches for infants and social security in old age.

*II. Labour Welfare*

Minimum wages and social security will be guaranteed to agricultural labour as also to all workers in the unorganised sectors of the economy. As for the industrial sector, the National Front will introduce progressive labour laws and promote workers' participation in the management of industries to create conditions in which industrial democracy could flourish. A rational wage policy will be formulated.

**Process of Action**

*Labour Participation in Management*

Workers and employers are partners in progress. To strengthen their united endeavour, the Government has introduced a Bill on Labour Participation in Management. The Bill envisages labour participation at the floor, management and board levels. The objective is to create an atmosphere conducive to bringing together employers and employees for increasing productivity. So far, the schemes for participation of workers in management have been non-statutory and have not been effective.

*Industrial Relations Bill*

In order to incorporate progressive measures in the Industrial Disputes Act, 1947, and the Trade Unions Act, 1926 the Government has set up a bipartite Committee comprising representatives of central trade union organisations and employers' organisations. The Committee is expected to submit its recommendations by July this year. The Industrial Relations Bill introduced by the previous government has been withdrawn.

As for the minimum wages for labourers, the Government has

decided that the minimum daily wage for labourers must be Rs 15 against Rs 11 prescribed earlier. The Centre has written to all State Governments to help in its implementation.

**Public Opinion**

Only some results.

LANGUAGE POLICY

**Promises and Precepts**

Use of regional languages in administration at State level and education at all levels shall be promoted. Pandit Nehru's assurance regarding language policy will be implemented and all efforts will be taken to promote Indian languages. Gujral Committee's recommendations on Urdu will be implemented. The Eighth Schedule will be extended to respond to the urges of other linguistic groups.

**Process of Action**

*Language Development and Three Language Formula*: On April 19, 1990, the Prime Minister V. P. Singh assured the members from the south that the Government would continue with the three-language formula.

Speaking after the Prime Minister, Minister of State incharge education, M. G. K. Menon said that it was natural for the Government to promote Indian languages. There were numerous programmes for it. As for Sanskrit, he said as many as 60 Universities offered it as a course and had departments for its teaching.

(*Hindustan Times*, April 19, 1990)

**Public Opinion**

No tangible results.

LICENSING POLICY

**Promises and Precepts**

Adhocism in licensing is at the root of all commercial corruption.

Long-term licensing policies will be announced for various sectors of industry and the entire procedure will be freed from both political favouritism and bureaucratic arbitrariness.

**Process of Action**

Following provisions have been made regarding licensing:

— To increase competitive edge of Indian manufactures, medium-sized investments to be freed from avoidable regulations.
— New units with investments up to Rs 25 crore in fixed assets in non-backward and Rs 75 crore in centrally-notified backward areas exempted from licensing/registration.
— Import entitlement of capital goods allowed up to 30 per cent (landed value) of total value of plant and machinery required by the unit.
— Imports of raw materials and components allowed up to landed value of 30 per cent of the ex-factory value of annual production.
— Simplification of procedures relating to technology transfer agreements.
— Delicensing of all export-oriented units and new units in export processing zones up to an investment of Rs 75 crore.
— Clearance requirement to be continued in the case of new units set up by companies covered under Monopolies and Restrictive Trade Practices and Foreign Exchange Regulation Act.

## MINIMUM NEEDS

**Promises and Precepts**

Through a major programme of employment generation and asset creation, the National Front will achieve its declared goal of fulfilling the essential minimum needs of the people.

**Process of Action**

No tangible results.

# MINORITIES

## Promises and Precepts

### *I. Minorities: Religious and Ethnic*

Religious and ethnic minorities will have the fullest protection in pursuing their modes of worship, following their personal laws and developing their institutions. Communal disturbances shall be prevented and firmly put down, when they occur. Educational and employment opportunities for the minorities will receive special attention.

### *II. Protection of Rights of Minorities*

Religious minorities will enjoy the fullest protection and opportunity to pursue their modes of worship and their religious beliefs and practices, and develop their institutions, whether religious, cultural, educational or welfare-oriented. Complete non-interference will be observed in their personal laws, their cultural advancement and fulfilment of their distinctive cultural identities.

The tragic recurrence of communal riots during the past five years has gained momentum in the Congress (I) States, killing large numbers of people in places like Kota, Badayun and Indore. Communal riots shall be strongly put down by effective prohibition of incitement of communal passions and by pursuing appropriate recruitment policies in police services and by creating mixed anti-riot force so as to ensure totally impartial conduct from them. Full compensation to victims of communal and caste riots will be provided. Action will be taken against officers who fail to control riots. Special courts will be constituted to try cases relating to communal and caste riots. Justice will be done to the victims of November 1984 riots in Delhi and elsewhere and those responsible will be punished.

The Minority Commission will be given statutory status.

In order to remove unemployment and economic backwardness among the minorities, the Government would take, *inter alia* the following steps:

1. Setting up Minorities Financial Corporations.
2. Representation for minorities on various recruitment

Committees and Boards.

3. Encouragement for establishment of technical and polytechnic institutions by minorities.
4. Preservation of the minority character of the educational institutions guaranteed under the Constitution.

**Process of Action**

A Cabinet committee under the Chairmanship of the Prime Minister has been set up for minorities for monthly monitoring of the implementation of the 15-Point Programme for Welfare of Minorities. A decision has been taken to set up Special Courts to try communal offences. Such Courts have already been set up in Delhi and Meerut. Action has been initiated to set up Special Courts in Bhagalpur, Indore and Kota.

Among the measures, mention may be made of proposals to launch programmes for acquisition of skills by minorities in minority concentration areas; imparting of training in trades relevant to minorities by ITI's; imparting of pre-examination training to enable minorities to compete on equal terms in competitive examinations for entry into professional colleges and for public service recruitment; and setting up of more bank branches in minority concentration areas to increase access to credit.

The scheme of compensation to victims of communal riots has been reworked. *Ex gratia* relief payment in cases of death or permanent incapacitation fixed at Rs 20,000 in 1983 has been raised to Rs 50,000. Effective from April 1990, pension of Rs 500 p.m. will be paid to widows of riot victims with low incomes.

NATIONAL RECONCILIATION

**Promises and Precepts**

Conflict, violence and confrontation have divided and hurt the nation during the past five years. This must end. A climate of tolerance and fraternity among all social groups must grow. Reconciliation through dialogue is the need of the hour. It shall be our foremost endeavour to bring about national reconciliation and provide the healing touch.

**Process of Action**

National Integration Council revived.

**Public Opinion**

*The Hindustan Times*, in its editorial dated April 13, 1990, detailed the role of the National Integration Council as, "There can only be limited expectations from the reconstituted National Integration Council mainly because it has neither the political clout nor the administrative authority to cope with all the divisive forces which have emerged in different parts of the country. The problem cannot be solved by merely passing a resolution against communalism or secessionism or by stressing the need for national unity. Things have gone from bad to worse in recent months to such an extent that mere platitudes serve no purpose. Nevertheless, the decision of the council to appoint a committee for drawing up an action plan to combat communalism and secessionism is significant, provided the plan is well thought out and comprehensive. Those who have attended the council meeting represent a cross-section of society, including personalities in various walks of life. The consensus at the meeting is that all-out efforts should be made to check the divisive forces although there may be differences on the strategy to be adopted. The issues that have figured prominently in the discussions are the escalation in terrorist violence in Punjab, the anti-national activities of secessionists in the Kashmir Valley, the emergence of forces of separatism in Assam and the increase in communal tension in the country."

The National Integration Council which met at Madras on September 26, 1990, failed to have useful discussions on Kashmir, Punjab and Assam issues. The B.J.P. had boycotted the meeting.

NATURAL RESOURCES AND ENVIRONMENT

**Promises and Precepts**

Since Independence, we have witnessed India rapidly deteriorate from one of the world's richest naturally endowed nations to a progressively growing waste land. During this period the country lost almost half of the forests which provided the people's daily needs of food, fodder, fuel, timber, herbs, medicines, fibre, fruits and variety of other essential utility items. Another consequence of deforestation is the severe depletion of groundwater resources.

With the majority of the countrymen still being poor, the degradation of the environment is leading to the degradation of the resource base on which alone the basic needs of people can be met.

To stop the degradation and the consequent forced rural exodus, the National Front will make the regeneration of the nation's resource base a priority area of the State Policy.

The National Front Government will ensure strict implementation of the pollution control laws.

### Process of Action

Action has been initiated in the conservation of natural resources and protection of environment from pollution.

## NUCLEAR POLICY

### Promises and Precepts

While committing itself to the peaceful uses of nuclear energy India cannot ignore the proximity of nuclear weapon and non-nuclear weapon powers in the region and must take that into account in evolving her security doctrine and it must keep its options open. The National Front Government will work for removal of the discriminatory clauses of the NPT.

### Process of Action

No tangible results.

## OLD AND THE HANDICAPPED

### Promises and Precepts

The old, the destitute and the physically handicapped will be specially looked after by providing them social security. Old age pensions will be guaranteed to all persons above the age of 60 years, who might otherwise be left uncared for and vulnerable, and they will be provided with cereals at subsidised rates and minimum cloth requirement. All the pensioners drawing Rs 500 or below per month will also be made eligible for these benefits.

**Process of Action**

No tangible results.

## PANCHAYAT RAJ

**Promises and Precepts**

The National Front is committed to promote a genuine devolution of powers, functions and resources of Panchayati Raj Institutions enabling the fullest participation of the people in the development process. The discredited attempts made by Rajiv government to bypass the States through legislative measures in the name of decentralization, will be replaced by genuine decentralization based on a national consensus.

The National Front will provide a legal guarantee to ensure regular elections to Panchayati Raj Institutions. It will secure, with the cooperation of the States, adequate representations in these bodies for Scheduled Castes, Scheduled Tribes, Backward classes and Women and devolution of financial and administrative powers.

**Process of Action**

*Constitutional Status*

Proposals on the subject were outlined before the Conference of Chief Ministers in June 1990, Prime Minister V.P. Singh had described them as a first step in the direction of turning 'Independence to Freedom'. The scheme provides for a flexible framework, with greater choice to State governments to modify it to suit local needs.

## PARLIAMENTARY DEMOCRACY

**Promises and Precepts**

The Front is pledged to revitalise the parliamentary institutions and to make them accountable to the people. The National Front will defend and strengthen, through appropriate reforms, the independence of judiciary and institutions like the C&AG and the Election Commission.

**Public Opinion**

*Karnataka Action Deplored*

. . . Another casualty of the cynical political drama is the prestige of the office of the Governor, as Shri Bhanu Pratap Singh overstepped the limits of his constitutional role in an obvious bid to foil the Congress-I game plan. Neither the Governor's laboured explanations nor the clarification of the Prime Minister that the "temporary imposition" of President's rule was done to resolve the constitutional crisis will dispel the impression that when it comes to misusing the gubernatorial office, the National Front is no different from the Congress-I. The uproar it caused in the country, with the National Front allies also joining in the criticism, may account for the Governor's promise to PCC-I chief Oscar Fernandes to set in motion the process for the revocation of President's rule and Shri V.P. Singh's assurance that it will be expedited with "the minimum of delay". The Centre's eagerness to undo the damage should not, however, obscure the fact that the Union Cabinet had no compunctions in endorsing the Governor's report, that too on a day when the Sarkaria Commission's recommendations on the topic were being discussed. But for the Governor's needless interference and his preposterous stipulation that the choice of the new leader has to be unanimous, it is doubtful whether Shri Bangarappa could have emerged as the consensus candidate even after the three-day exertions by the observers. All in all, neither the Congress-I nor the National Front has come out clean from the Karnataka imbroglio, which seems to have left only Shri Patil unscathed in terms of political morality.

(Editorial, *Hindustan Times*, October 15, 1990)

As expected, the hasty and indefensible imposition of President's rule in Karnataka has recoiled heavily on the ruling National Front Government at the Centre. With Shri S. Bangarappa unanimously elected leader of the Congress(I) Legislature Party in the State and the Governor, Shri Bhanu Pratap Singh, having recommended the revocation of President's rule which had earlier been imposed at his behest, the Congress(I) has succeeded in having its fortunes restored in the State. On the other hand the National Front Government's claim of being an upholder of norms and values in politics has suffered yet another dent.

(Editorial, *Indian Express*, October 17, 1990)

## POLITICAL PROBLEMS

### Promises and Precepts

*I. Assam*

In respect of Assam, full and expenditious implementation of the Assam Accord shall be ensured. Utmost care will be taken to ensure that there is no injustice or harassment to genuine Indian citizens. The National Front Government shall not allow any further division of Assam and the tribal problem will be settled through dialogue and negotiations.

*II. Jammu and Kashmir*

No specific mention.

*III. Punjab*

The National Front Government will immediately take steps to resolve the Punjab tangle. Laws that violate civil liberties will be reviewed. All those prisoners against whom there are no specific charges will be released. Wide-ranging discussions will be held, without preconditions, with leaders of various sections of the people for a political solution to the Punjab problem. A round-table Conference will be convened for this purpose. Elections to the Punjab Assembly will be held expeditiously. Discussions between Punjab, Haryana and Rajasthan for settlement of disputes will be organised.

### Process of Action

*I. Assam*

In Assam, the agitation of All Bodo Students Union demanding a separate State has been suspended following the talks held in New

Delhi between the agitators and the State Government. But the terrorist activities of the United Liberation Front of Assam (ULFA) are causing much concern. The State Government has been advised to take effective measures to give protection to the people and take effective security measures. Meetings to sort out matters have also been held.

*II. Jammu & Kashmir*

In Jammu & Kashmir, the stepped up violent activities of subversive elements and terrorists, with incitement and involvement from across the border, have complicated the issue. The opposition was taken into confidence and an all-party delegation visited Kashmir. The Government has also declared its readiness to meet any situation that may arise out of the involvement of Pakistan in this matter. At the same time, all measures are being taken to carry on with the administrative and developmental tasks.

The State of Jammu and Kashmir came under President's Rule with effect from the night of July 18, after the expiry of six months' Governor's rule which was promulgated on January 19 after Dr. Farooq Abdullah had resigned as Chief Minister of the State. This was for the second time that the State was being brought under President's Rule. According to a President's Rule. According to a Presidential notification, the President has assumed all the functions. The proclamation has been issued under Article 356 of the Constitution of India.

*Kashmir Declared Disturbed Area*

The Jammu and Kashmir Governor, Shri Girish Chander Saxena, declared on July 5, 1990, all the six districts of Kashmir Valley as 'disturbed area'.

*J & K Armed Forces Ordinance*

Governor Shri Saxena, on July 6, promulgated the Armed Forces, (Jammu & Kashmir) Special Power Ordinance, 1990. The Act gives special powers to the armed forces to carry out searches and destroy hideouts of militants in the entire Kashmir Valley and a 20 km belt from the line of actual control in the border districts of Poonch and Rajouri in Jammu region.

*III. Punjab*

* The Government has unveiled a four pronged strategy to deal with terrorists' and secessionists' activities in Punjab and Jammu and Kashmir. This involves.

- Firm security measures against terrorist violence;
- Free hand for Governors of these two States to deal with the problem;
- Fairness with the people;
- Continuous efforts to involve the people and to carry forward political initiatives.

The Prime Minister, along with some of his Cabinet colleagues, paid a goodwill visit to the Golden Temple soon after assuming office. A four member Cabinet Committee on Punjab was formed. An all-party meeting was held in New Delhi on December 17, 1989 where a broad consensus was reached to evolve a fresh approach to the problem. An all-party rally was held at Ludhiana where a resolution condemning violence and calling for the creation of a congenial atmosphere was adopted. The Prime Minister, his Cabinet colleagues and a number of leaders of various political parties, while paying homage to martyrs at Jallianwala Bagh on the Baisakhi Day, i.e., 13th April, pledged to work for a secular, united India.

** The 75th Constitutional Amendment Bill designed to extend President's Rule in Punjab by another six months fell through in the Lok Sabha on October 1, 1990. The Bill received 249 votes in favour and three against in a House with an effective total strength of 525 including the Speaker. The opposition Congress-I refused to participate in the voting on the ground that it was the main responsibility of the Government to ensure simple majority.

*** On October 4, 1990, both the Houses approved the Bill regarding extension of the President's Rule in Punjab for another six months up to November 10, 1991. The same day the Bill got the assent of the President.

## Public Opinion

### *Punjab*

*Government Inaction on Punjab Decried*: Members of the Lok Sabha severely criticised and condemned the latest statement of Shri Simranjit Singh Mann expressing his resolve to fight for a separate State of Khalistan. The members urged the Government to step up action against the terrorists and secessionist forces in Punjab.

Raising the issue during the zero hour, Congress-I member Kamal Nath wanted to know what the Government was going to do against the Akali Dal (Mann) move to write tot the UN for supervising the election in Punjab whenever it is held next.

Criticising Shri Mann's statement for a separate State, Shri Nath referred to his continued absence in the House. Supported by his party colleague Kamal Choudhary, he said the Parliamentary Committee on absence of members was in the process of submitting its report, and he wanted to know the Government reaction thereto.

CPM member Saifuddin Choudhary said Shri Mann's statement could only help thwart the political process the Government was planning to initiate. He pointed out that when the US ambassador visited Punjab on August 6, a group of AISSF activists submitted a memorandum asking for American support for achieving the Khalistani goal. He asked the Government to look into the issue.

BJP leader L.K. Advani said the Government had miscalculated about Shri Mann and it was futile to hold parleys with him. He added that the country and the Government were unable to understand what Shri Mann actually wanted. He called upon Shri Mann to make his stand clear.

Shri Advani said Shri Mann must be made to understand that the Government could negotiate with him only up to a point and not beyond. He wanted the Government to instil confidence among the Sikhs whom he described patriotic. He added that it was wrong on the part of the Government to treat Shri Mann as the key figure. In this context he referred to a statement of the Government criticising Shri Mann.

CPI member Geeta Mukherjee wanted the Government to assure the Sikh community of a fair play within the Union. But she warned the Government against yielding to the terrorists.

FB member Chitta Basu urged the House to condemn Shri Mann's latest statement. Appealing to the people of Punjab to isolate the secessionists, he said the attempts of the foreign human rights organisation to go to Punjab was an interference in the internal affairs of the country.

Akali (Mann) member Bimal Khalsa blamed the previous Government for everything that had gone wrong in Punjab. She said although the new Government attached top priority to Punjab, nothing had yet been done. She urged the Government to waive off the loan of Punjab farmers.

She said the Congress-I was responsible for making the Sikhs raise the Khalistan demand. She asked who were those responsible for the massacre of Sikhs in Delhi and elsewhere in 1984.

Smt. Khalsa said if the TV could be granted autonomy, she wondered why Punjab could not be granted the same. She wanted autonomy for all the States.

When she referred to a statement of Shri Rajiv Gandhi that whenever a big tree fell, the earth tremoured, several Congress-I members were up on their feet objecting to the reference.

BJP member Uma Bharati asked those who were pleading on behalf of terrorists to show courage and condemn the killings of innocent people as well as the demand for Khalistan. She felt that there was a need to encourage the people of Punjab to restore normal life.

Congress-I member Bhajan Lal referred to the grave situation in Punjab and defended the action taken by his party when in power. He added that the defenders of extremists should ask themselves who had desecrated the Golden Temple.

Another opposition member B. Shankaranand said the Government should consult other parties to hammer out a solution. He said while his party was blamed for all the wrong in Punjab, the new Government had not yet done anything concrete.

He felt the objective of the Prime Minister appeared to divert the attention of the people from one crisis to another because he did not have any solution.

(*Hindustan Times*, September 1, 1990)

Statistics prove that every extension of the President's rule has meant more killings and more suffering for the people of Punjab. Intellectuals who equate democracy with the mechanical process of vote casting are crying themselves hoarse for an election here and now. Our Prime Minister says: "One thing I will regret all my life is not holding elections within six months of the National Front Government coming to power."

(Jagjit Singh Anand, *Hindustan Times*, October 1, 1990)

*Economic Package*

The economic package announced by the Government among other things. The package, among other things, promises jobs to 100,000 youth under a self-employment scheme besides a special grant of Rs. 100 crores for human resource development. Of this Rs. 50 crores is for general education and Rs. 25 crores each for technical education and health. For the long-term economic development of the State, there is a proposal to set up a petrochemical complex and a string of sugar and cotton textile mills. Other peripheral provisions include recruitment of 10,000 Punjabi youth in army and paramilitary forces, extensive fencing of Punjab's border with Pakistan, and streamlining of immigration and customs facilities at Amritsar airport.

As observed by Hasan Suroor in an article 'Flip-flop over Punjab':

"An economic package announced by the Government was so timed as to give the impression of being calculated to 'buy' support — a cheque which the Government would probably cash when the elections are held six months from now. But why was not such a package announced earlier — say, after the last extension of President's rule? . . .

The package is hardly likely to provide an instant solution to Punjab's problems. Some may even see it as a sop — a case of being too late, and too little".

(*Frontline*, October 13 to 26, 1990)

The former Punjab Chief Minister Parkash Singh Badal who now heads the Akali Dal has described the economic package announced by the National Front Government as "an eye-wash, mirage and at best a dry carrot."

Punjab Governor Virendra Verma, however, described it as a big step to help Punjab. Shri Badal, however, said that the people of Punjab and particularly the Sikhs have lost all faith in the Central Government. "We find the Government headed by Shri V.P. Singh as utterly lacking in sincerity, devoid of any commitment for democracy and public good. Punjab has been once again denied to have an elected Government and the black Central rule has been forced on us," he told newsmen.

What is there in this so-called package? Does it touch the real issues for which Akalis and Punjabis have been agitating?, he asked. "The Government thinks that it could present this dry carrot and win the hearts and minds of the Punjabis to subjugation, while Punjab cried for political settlement of its issues and the nation to demonstrate its concern. All political parties have joined together to deny Punjab even an elected Government, he said.

Making one of the harshest criticism of the V.P. Singh Government, Shri Badal who had wished the Government well and had drawn a fine distinction between Shri Singh and Shri Rajiv Gandhi, said "people have no faith and the Government no credibility. It lacks any political sense to resolve issues and the country is facing worst crisis since independence." He said Prime Minister's promise to punish the guilty of November 1984 riots against the Sikhs and honourable settlement of the army deserters lay belied to this day so what use of having faith in him.

Shri Badal felt that this kind of deceptive politics always gave birth to violence and militancy and this is what is happening around the country.

He rejected the idea of advisory council by saying, "if the Governor's writ does not run in the State, what small this body without any constitutional sanctions achieve. We are not for this game," he declared.

Shri Badal warned against this kind of approach to the problems of Punjab or that of the nation. "It seems in Punjab all other parties believe in looting. There is no law and there is no Government here," he said.

Shri Badal said his party leaders who are to meet here on October 12 shall take, stock of the situation and decide their line of action. He said that there is a clear mood to have more cohesion with the militants and the statement of the party general secretaries is a good one. But Shri Badal refused to comment whether he agreed with the demand made by Shri Simranjit Singh Mann that since the present Government was insincere, there should be vote on right of self-determination under the United Nations. He left to his partymen to consider anything. He appealed to the Akalis of all hues to join hands and defeat this nefarious game of denying Punjab even an elected Government, much less a democratic process and honourable place.

(*Hindustan Times*, October 7, 1990)

## POLITICAL TASKS

*See*

Administrative Structure: Responsive Administrative Structure
Civil Liberties Corruption: Curbing Corruption
Democratic Rights: Electoral Reforms
Judiciary: Independence of Judiciary
Minorities: Protection of Rights of Minorities
Panchayat Raj
Political Problems: Solution to Political Problems: Assam, Jammu & Kashmir, Punjab
Ram Janam Bhoomi/Babri Masjid
Regional Aspirations
Right to Information
Union-State Relations

## PRICE RISE ARRESTING

### Promises and Precepts

The annual double digit rate of inflation and spiralling prices of essential commodities during the 6th and 7th Plan periods have affected the common man adversely and jeopardised the entire development process. The worst hit are the rural poor as is obvious from the escalation in the cost of living index for the agricultural labour. The National Front considers price stability as crucial for removal of poverty and steady growth of economy.

Abnormal price rise will be checked by firm control on deficit financing and inflation, strict enforcement of financial discipline, austerity in public expenditure and progressive reduction in non-development expenditure. The public distribution system will be strengthened and expanded to cover all the vulnerable sections of the society so that cereals, sugar, edible oils, standard cloth and other daily household needs are supplied at fair prices. Stringent action shall be taken against hoarders and blackmarketeers. Consumer protection and cooperative marketing will be encouraged.

### Process of Action

The Prime Minister has written to the Chief Ministers of all the States and Union Territories sharing the serious concern about the general price situation and seeking their assistance and cooperation in the matter.

He has requested the Chief Ministers to streamline and rejuvenate the Public Distribution System and to ruthlessly bring to book hoarders and economic offenders artificially raising prices of essential commodities.

As for the essential commodities, specific and firm measures have been initiated to check their price rise. Central Ministries concerned have been directed to constantly keep a watch on the situation and take prompt remedial measures. Some of the measures taken include:

- Traders warned, 25000 raids conducted against hoarders during past four months.
- Release of more quantities of levy sugar and edible oils through the Public Distribution System.
- Bank Credit against oil/oilseed stocks restricted to prevent hoarding. Stock limits on edible oil with traders reduced.
- Tea exports staggered to ease domestic supply.
- On Government's initiative, cement producers agree to bring down cement prices to the level prevailing on March 31, 1990.

The pressure of inflation is clearly linked to fiscal imbalance. The budgetary deficit as on December 1, 1989 was Rs. 13,790 crore, a level nearly double the deficit projected for the whole year in the 1989-90 budget. This year the Government has decided to go in for hard measures to get to the root of the problem by controlling the deficit at a far lower level of around Rs. 7,200 crore.

The country's oil consumption has been rising at the rate of around 8 per cent in the recent past. One-sixth of the import bill is on this account. Reversing this trend and curtailing external borrowing so as to preserve our economic freedom would be possible only through the hard measures such as the recent hike in petroleum prices. It may be unsavoury in the short run, but it will save the nation from a possible debt trap.

As for the fiscal policy, the tax structure is being simplified with more incentives for industrial growth. The 1990-91 budget extended a number of concessions to stimulate growth and help the small scale sector. The Finance Minister, in his budget speech, emphasised the need to make tax system more stable and predictable. With this end in view the Government is to present long-term fiscal policy later this year.

### Public Opinion

*B.J.P. Leader A.B. Vajpayee*

Bharatiya Janata Party leader Atal Behari Vajpayee took the National Front Government to task in the Rajya Sabha when he accused it of having miserably failed to control the rising prices, a promise which had been made in their manifesto.

"What we see today is the skyrocketing prices and a Government which is incapable of putting a stop to this unique phenomenon. Nobody could deny that the country today was caught up in a cobweb of rising prices with little hope of halting the upward swing," he said.

Shri Vajpayee was initiating a short duration discussion on the rising prices, a notice for which had been given, by 42 members belonging to almost all the parties including the ruling party.

He said, ironically the National Front Government was today caught on two fronts, viz. on the question of moral values and on the issue of rising prices. The country's economy was in shambles, which it had inherited from the previous Government. But as soon as the National Front Government had come to power, it had made a solemn promise that its first task would be to control prices.

Shri Vajpayee regretted that although the Prime Minister had written letters to the State Chief Ministers and urged them to take all possible steps to control rising prices, yet nothing tangible had been achieved. Inflation is galloping and the price situation was far from satisfactory. In order to authenticate his allegations, Shri Vajpayee marshalled out facts and figures about the increase in the prices of essential commodities. Not only retail but even wholesale prices had gone up which was rather unprecedented. Steps that Government had taken were inadequate, Shri Vajpayee said.

On the question of edible oil prices, Shri Vajpayee deplored that the Government had been crying from the housetops that it would not import edible oils thereby giving a singal to the traders to increase prices. What the Government should have done was to announce that as and when there was a rise in edible oil prices, it would intervene and import whatever quantity was required. This would have acted as a damper on the traders.

But the Government had made it clear that there would be no imports and, therefore, the prices have gone sky high with a little hope of their coming down, the BJP leader said. It was not Newton's law that operated in the case of prices. Once the prices have gone up there was little change of these coming down. How was it that cement was being sold at Rs. 80 at the Super Bazar and at Rs. 90 and Rs. 100 per bag in the open market, he asked.

Shri Vajpayee also said that Government must ensure a link between the cost prices and the sale prices. In the case of scooters, according to his information, the cost prices, including 20 per cent profit margin, was around Rs. 7,000 but the market price was Rs. 12,000. A toothbrush cost price was Re. 1.10, but it was being sold for Rs. 3.50. Why, he asked. Why does not the Government look into this aspect and restrain the profiteers from fleecing the consumers, Shri Vajpayee demanded.

Shri Vajpayee wanted that the Government should put some limit on borrowings. According to his information, Rs. 120 crore is the daily debt of the Government. What success had the Government made in curbing its expenditure? Why was the debt increasing? Government must place the whole figures before the House, he said. There had to be economic discipline. The State electricity boards owed Rs. 800 crore to the Railways.

There should be remunerative prices to the farmers, but the consumers too should not be fleeced. Farmers are also consumers and whatever they get by way of higher prices is taken away by the rising prices, the leader said.

Shri Vajpayee in anguish remarked that sometimes "he felt that all Governments are alike. In the past, the previous Government was working like this, and now the National Front Government was doing the same thing".

*Congress-I Former Finance Minister S.B. Chavan*

Former Finance Minister S.B. Chavan said that his party was not interested in the ouster of the National Front Government, but it was the ruling party which had brought about the present price situation.

He said it was wrong to repeatedly say that the National Front Government had inherited the present situation from the previous Government. If one compared the prices that ruled in December 1989 and May 1990, the difference would be quite revealing. There had been unprecedented increase in the prices of all commodities. The National Front had held out an assurance to the people that it would keep the prices under control. But, unfortunately, it had miserably failed because prices have increased on all fronts.

Shri Chavan said the Government should maintain a link between the cost of production and the prices at which the consumers got various commodities.

(*Hindustan Times*, August 7, 1990).

## PUBLIC SECTOR AND PRIVATE ENTERPRISE

### Promises and Precepts

The Public Sector shall be freed from excessive bureaucratisation, inefficiency and underutilisation of capacity, while the private corporate sector shall be freed from the rigours of unnecessary and excessive controls. The National Front shall strengthen both these sectors so that they can reduce the role of multinationals in Indian economy, subserve the needs of agriculture, develop and provide appropriate technology for cottage and small scale sector, activate import substitution and push up exports in a big way in order to achieve the goal of national self-reliance. The National Front shall make all necessary adjustments in taxation and credit policies to ensure that they achieve these goals and also respond to the growing market in the rural sector, which will be the obvious consequence of the altered strategy of economic development.

### Process of Action

No tangible results.

## RAM JANAM BHOOMI/BABRI MASJID ISSUE

### Promises and Precepts

The Babri Masjid/Ram Janam Bhoomi controversy has become a matter of grave anxiety to the people of the country. The Union Government, by its inaction and sometimes by deliberate instigation by the Congress(I) State Government, has allowed this sore to fester. It is the firm belief of the National Front that the controversy can be settled through negotiations, based upon mutual understanding.

The National Front feels that the Babri Masjid should not be demolished. At the same time, the Hindu sentiments to have a temple dedicated to Lord Rama should be respected.

The National Front feels that an amicable settlement on the above lines can be found. No precipitate action should be taken by any group pending such settlement or a decision by the Court.

## Process of Action

### *I. Text of President's Ordinance (19-10-1990)*

The following is the text of the Ram Janma Bhumi-Babri Masjid. (Acquisition of Area) Ordinance, 1990:

Promulgated by the President in the Forty-first year of the Republic of India.

An Ordinance to provide for the acquisition of the Ram Janma Bhumi-Babri Masjid area and for matters connected therewith or incidental thereto.

Whereas Parliament is not in session and the President is satisfied that circumstances exist which render it necessary for him to take immediate action.

Now, therefore, in exercise of the powers conferred by Clause (I) of Article 123, of the Constitution, the President is pleased to promulgate the following Ordinance:

CHAPTER I

*Preliminary*

1. (1) This Ordinance may be called the Ram Janma Bhumi-Babri Masjid (Acquisition of Area) Ordinance 1990.

   (2) It shall come into force at once.

2. In this Ordinance, unless the context otherwise requires,

   (a) "area" means the area (including all the buildings, structure or other properties;

   (b) "authorised person" means a person or body of persons appointed by the Central Government under Sub-section (1) of

Section 7.

## CHAPTER II

*Acquisition of Ram Janma Bhumi-Babri Masjid Area*

3. On and from the commencement of this Ordinance, the rights, title and interest in relation to the Ram Janma Bhumi-Babri Masjid area, as specified in the Schedule, shall, by virtue of this Ordinance, stand transferred to, and vest in, the Central Government.

4. (1) The area shall be deemed to include all assets, rights, leaseholds, powers, authority and privileges and all property, movable and immovable, including lands, buildings, structure, shops of whatever nature or other properties and all other rights and interests arising out of such properties as were immediately before the commencement of this Ordinance in the ownership, possession, power or control of any person and all registers, maps, plans, drawings, records of survey and other documents of whatever nature relating thereto.

(2) All properties aforesaid which have vested in the Central Government under Section 3 shall, by force of such vesting, be freed and discharged from any trust obligation, mortgage, charge, lien and all other encumbrances affecting them and any attachment, injunction, decree of order of any court or tribunal or other authority restricting the use of such properties in any manner or appointing any receiver in respect of the whole or any part of such properties shall be deemed to have been withdrawn.

(3) If, on the commencement of this Ordinance, any suit, appeal or other proceeding, of whatever nature, in relation to any property which has vested in the Central Government under Section (3), is pending before any court, tribunal or other authority , the same shall abate.

5. (1) The Central Government may take all necessary steps to secure possession of the area which is vested in that Government under Section 3.

(2) On the vesting of the area in the Central Government under Section 3, the person in charge of the management of the area immediately before such vesting shall be bound to deliver to the

Central Government or the authorised person, all assets, registers and other documents in their custody relating to such area.

6. (1) Notwithstanding anything contained in Clause (B) of Section 2 and Section 3, 4, 5 and 7, the Central Government may, if it is satisfied that any authority or body is willing to comply or has complied with such terms and conditions as the Government may think fit to impose, direct by notification, that the right, title and interest in relation to the area or any part thereof shall, instead of continuing of vest in the Central Government, vest in that authority or body either on the date of the notification or on such earlier or later date (not being a date earlier than the commencement of this Ordinance) as may be specified in the notification.

(2) When the right, title and interest in relation to the area or part thereof vest in the authority or body referred to in Sub-section (1), all the rights of the Central Government in relation to such area or part shall, on and from the date of such vesting, be deemed to have become the rights of that authority or body.

(3) The provision of Clause (B) of Section 2, and Section 3, 4, 5, 7 and 10 shall, so far as may be, apply in relation to such authority or body as they apply in relation to the Central Government and for this purpose references therein to the "Central Government" shall be construed as references to such authority or body.

## CHAPTER III

*Management and Administration of Property*

7. (1) Notwithstanding anything contained in any contract or instrument or order of any court, tribunal or, other authority to the contrary, on and from the commencement of this Ordinance, the property vested in the Central Government under Section 3 shall be managed by the Central Government or by a person or body of persons authorised by that Government in this behalf.

(2) In managing the property vested in the Central Government under Section 3, the Central Government or the authorised person shall ensure that the position existing immediately before the commencement of this Ordinance is maintained.

## CHAPTER IV

*Miscellaneous*

8. (1) The owner of any land, building, structure of other property comprised in the area specified in the Schedule shall be given by the Central Government, for the transfer to and vesting in that Government under Section 3 of that land, building, structure or other property, in cash an amount equivalent to the market value of the land, building, structure or other property.

(2) The owner or any person having a claim against the owner may make a claim to the Central Government or to a person authorised by the Government in that behalf within a period of 90 days from the date of commencement of this Ordinance:

Provided that if the Central Government or the person so authorised is satisfied that the claimant was prevented by sufficient cause from preferring the claim within the said period of 90 days, the Central Government or the person so authorised may entertain the claim within a further period of 90 days and not thereafter.

9. The provisions of this Ordinance shall have effect notwithstanding anything inconsistent therewith contained in any other law for the time being in force or any instrument having effect by virtue of any law other than this Ordinance or any decree or order of any court, tribunal or other authority.

10. No, suit, prosecution or other legal proceeding shall be against the Central Government, authorised person or any of the officers or other employees of that Government or person for anything which is in good faith done or intended to be done under this Ordinance.

11. Notwithstanding anything contained in the Code of Criminal Procedure, 1973, no court shall take cognizance of any offence under the Ordinance except on a complaint, in writing, made by the Central Government or any officer authorised in this behalf by that Government.

12. (1) The Central Government may, by notification in the Official Gazette, make rules to carry our the provisions of this Ordinance.

(2) Every rule made by the Central Government under this

Ordinance shall be laid, as soon as may be after it is made, before each House of Parliament, while it is in session, for a total period of 30 days which may be comprised in one session or in two or more successive sessions, and if, before the expiry of the session immediately following the session or the successive sessions aforesaid, both Houses agree in making any modification in the rule or both Houses agree that the rule should not be made, the rule shall thereafter have effect only in such modified form or be of no effect, as the case may be; so, however, that any such modification or annulment shall be without prejudice to the validity of anything previously done under the rule.

## THE SCHEDULE

[*See Sections 2(a), 3 and 8*]

*Description of Area*

All land, buildings, structures and other properties comprised in the area situated in village Kot Ramchandar in Ayodhya in the district of Faizabad of the State of Uttar Pradesh and bounded as follows;

In the North — by the road which links Hanuman Garhi with Druahi Kunwa,
In the South — by Khasra plot No. 172.
In the East — by Khasra plot Nos. 1105, 1106 and 1118.
In the West — by the road in Nazul plot No. 577.

*II. Stay of Implementation*

On October 21, 1990, the Union Government stayed the implementation of the ordinance issued on October 19, 1990, in view of its rejection by Vishwa Hindu Parishad and Babri Masjid Action Committee.

*III. Three-Point Formula of the Government on Temple Issue*

On October 19, 1990 the Union Government offered a compromise formula to resolve the controversial Ramjanambhoomi-Babri Masjid dispute under which the mosque shall be retained in the present form while the construction of the temple can be started side by side.

The proposal also suggests that the dispute may be referred to the

Supreme Court for expeditious disposal under a presidential reference as provided for in Article 143 of the Constitution.

This was announced on October 19, 1990 at a Press conference by Minister for Parliamentary Affairs P. Upendra. He said that the formula had been evolved after holding detailed discussions during the last few days with the concerned parties, religious leaders and prominent publicmen.

The three-point formula proposes that the Government may acquire the land under dispute before the Lucknow bench of the Allahabad High Court and other appurtenant land. The number two point suggests that barring such disputed land in dispute before the Court, the other acquired area may be made available to Ramjanmabhoomi Samiti or (Niyas) which is agitating for the construction of the temple for building the same.

Point three of the formula suggests that the dispute presently under consideration by the Court may be referred to the Supreme Court under Article 143, through a presidential reference for expeditious disposal of the case.

While the matter is before the Supreme Court, the Government will maintain *status quo* which implies that the *pooja* will continue in the disputed premises and and mosque shall not be demolished. The Minister announced that the Government is inclined to favourably respond to the above proposals and in case the parties concerned agree to the same, action would be taken on them.

### *IV. Temple Area Taken Over*

The Central Government on October 19, 1990 acquired the land in dispute before the Allahabad High Court regarding the Ram Janmabhoomi-Babri Masjid and other appurtenant area.

According to an ordinance promulgated by the President, the Ram Janmabhoomi-Babri Masjid dispute would be referred to the Supreme Court for expeditious disposal under Article 143 of the Constitution.

Pending decision of the Supreme Court, the Government would maintain *status quo* on the disputed area.

Barring such disputed land which was before the Allahabad High Court, the other acquired areas would be made available to the Ram Janma Yagya Samiti or Nyas (trust) for the construction of the Sri Ram Temple.

Article 143 says: "(1) If at any time it appears to the President that a question of law or fact has arisen, or is likely to arise, which is of such a nature and of such public importance that it is expedient to obtain the opinion of the Supreme Court upon it, he may refer to question to that court for consideration and the court may, after such hearing as it thinks fit, report to the President its opinion thereon.

"(2) The President may, notwithstanding anything in the provision to Article 131, refer a dispute of the kind mentioned in the said proviso to the Supreme Court for opinion and the Supreme Court shall after such hearing as it thinks fit, report to the President its opinion thereon."

*V. Security of Temple Taken Over*

The security of the Ramjanmabhoomi-Babri Masjid site in Ayodhya has been taken over by the Central Government following the acquisition of the disputed property and its adjoining areas through an ordinance.

The Faizabad Commissioner Madhukar Gupta has been appointed officer-in-charge of the acquired property in Ayodhya by the Centre. The security of the acquired property will be henceforth managed by the Commissioner in his capacity of officer in charge.

So far the security of the disputed shrine was managed by the State Government. The disputed site had been surrounded by thick iron bars at the time of "*shilanayas*" with a heavy deployment of forces for its security.

All the cases relating to the Ramjanmabhoomi-Babri Masjid pending with the High Court will be henceforth treated as closed. The Central will be referring these cases to the Supreme Court, as a part of a three-point formula prepared by the Government to resolve the dispute.

Earlier on the State Government's request a special three-member bench had been constituted for early disposal of the cases.

The Centre's decision of referring the cases to the Supreme Court had evoked mixed response. Though the State Government officials are apparently relaxed with the security of the disputed site being handed over to the Centre, legal experts wonder whether the Government of India has the right to acquire such a 'religious property'. They cite a verdict recently given by the High Court on the acquisition of *Dharmashalas* by the district magistrate in Ayodhaya.

The High Court had stayed the September 24 order of Faizabad district magistrate through which Kanack Bhawan, Manas Trust, Janaki Mahal, Jain Mandir and Birla Dharmashalas were to be acquired for the accommodation of police and officials.

The Government, opposing the writ petition filed by Shri Harishankar Jain, Secretary of the Vishwa Hindu Adhivakta Sangh, had stated that the "*Dharmashalas*" had been acquired following a written permission of their owners.

## Public Opinion

### *B.J.P.*

B.J.P. President L.K. Advani, described the proposal as one sought to "buy time" rejected the Centre's three-point formula on Ayodhya dispute, saying his party would not accept any solution which did not provide for the building of a temple at the birthplace of Ram at Ayodhya.

Shri Atal Behari Vajpayee said that the disputed area in Ayodhya should be declared as the "Ram Janmasthan" and handed over to the Ram Janmabhoomi Yagya Samiti. He said that although the Government had taken "a step in the right direction", the Centre would have to do more than that to make its proposals acceptable.

Dr. Murli Manohar Joshi pointed out at his Press conference, the Centre has also acquired the land which was "not" under a dispute so far, like the place where the *Shilanyas* was performed on November 9, 1989. This could come in the way of the construction of the temple there, he said.

The Bharatiya Janata Party described the Ordinance as a "very small step taken very late". Party general secretary Dr Murli Manohar Joshi, however, expressed regret at a Press briefing that the Ordinance suffered from "several infirmities" as the main question with regard to the Janmasthan, the *sanctum sanctorum* of the proposed temple, remained unresolved.

### *Congress-I President Rajiv Gandhi*

On the three-point formula put forward by the Centre for solving the Ram Janmabhoomi-Babri Masjid issue, Shri Gandhi said 'there is not need to comment on it as the concerned parties have already rejected it'.

He said it was now up to the government to come out with an acceptable solution.

He reiterated the Congress-I stand that the dispute should be solved through a negotiated settlement or await the court verdict, which should be observed. In the meantime the *status quo* should be maintained.

*National Front Former Deputy Prime Minister Devi Lal*

Welcomed the Government's initiative in coming out with the three-point formula on the Ram Janmabhoomi-Babri Masjid issue and the ordinance which has been promptly issued for acquiring the disputed land at Ayodhya.

*Babri Masjid Action Committee*

The Babri Masjid Action Committee on October 20, 1990 gave a call for the "Bharat Bandh" on October 30 to protest against the ordinance issued by the President on to resolve the Ram Janmabhoomi-Babri Masjid dispute and demanded immediate withdrawal of the ordinance.

Mr. Salahuddin Owaisi, MP and chairman of the action committee, alleged that the three-point formula announced by the Government went against the resolution of the all-party meeting. The Action Committee rejected the formula.

*Babri Masjid Coordination Committee*

The Babri Masjid Coordination Committee, rejected the Government formula. It demanded that the Government should facilitate an early verdict on the matter by the Lucknow bench of the High Court.

*National Front Chairman N.T. Rama Rao*

National Front Chairman N.T. Rama Rao hailed the Government's three-point formula to resolve the Ram Janmabhoomi-Babri Masjid issue and appealed to the Vishwa Hindu Parishad (VHP) to positively respond to it "in the interest of communal harmony and for the greater glory of our motherland".

In a statement, Shri Rama Rao, said the decision to acquire the disputed land and to refer the dispute to the Supreme Court "is the only solution to the current impasse."

"All people who have the country's interest uppermost in their minds should come out in support of the three-point formula announced by the Government," he said and referred to the discussions he had held in the last couple of days with leaders of the BJP and other parties that had "helped the Government to evolve the three-point formula".

The Prime Minister and Shri Rama Rao, are understood to have taken stock of the situation, particularly in the context of the VHP's total rejection of the formula proposed by the Government last night. It was in this context that Shri Rama Rao issued a statement subsequently, urging the VHP to respond positively to the Government's initiative.

Mr. Rama Rao, expressed the hope that the VHP even at this stage would come round. Shri Rama Rao said the VHP could still go ahead with its "kar seva" for building the Ram temple at the "undisputed land" near the structures in dispute.

"Let us wait and see", he said when asked if a settlement could be brought about with this formula, in view of the VHP's stance. He declined to comment on whether the Government might have to go a little further to accommodate the viewpoint of VHP and BJP. According to him, there is no better solution them the formula offered by the Government in the present circumstances.

(*Hindustan Times*, October 20, 1990)

*Congress-S*

The Congress-S, welcoming the Government's decision to acquire the Ram Janmabhoomi-Babri Masjid and other appurtenant areas in dispute, said the three-point formula should allay the apprehensions of all those who were feeling that the Central Government was not doing enough "to stall the progress of the unfortunate Rath Yatra".

Mr. I.P. Singh, general secretary of the Congress-S, said that the Government's initiative was a matter of deep gratification to all secular forces in the country. The Congress-S, he said, had right from the beginning been advocating firm steps "to stem the tide of communal frenzy", in the wake of the Rath yatra.

*Left Parties*

The CPI, CPI-M and other Left parties today welcomed the three-point formula announced by the Government to resolve the Ram Janmabhoomi-Babri Masjid discord.

They held a joint meeting here and said in a joint statement that the Vishwa Hindu Parishad, BJP and others should accept the formula and give up the path of confrontation and avert communal conflagration.

The statement appreciated that the ordinance issued by the President stipulated that the temple could be built on an undisputed plot of land which Government might give to the VHP in Ayodhya.

The statement however advised the Government to see that all parties to the dispute got an opportunity to represent their views before the Supreme Court, when it took up the matter under Article 143 of the Constitution, and that the terms of reference should be carefully framed by the Government.

*Vishwa Hindu Parishad*

The Vishwa Hindu Parishad (VHP) has unequivocally rejected the three-point formula evolved by the Government during the day-long parleys on October 19, 1990 for a solution to the Ram Janmabhoomi issue.

"No understanding is possible till the small, 80 feet by 40 feet piece of land (the "janmasthan") is handed over to us," VHP general secretary Ashok Singhal told.

The entire dispute was for this piece of land only and the countrywide agitation had been launched to obtain possession of this land. There would be no compromise on this.

The Government might give the entire Ayodhya or even the universe. but all that the VHP sought was that particular piece of land where Lord Ram was born.

(*Hindustan Times*, October 19, 1990)

*Janta Dal Leader Chandra Shekhar*

Janata Dal leader Chandra Shekhar said the three-point formula suggested by the Government to resolve the Ram Janmabhoomi-Babri Masjid controversy was "unintelligible" to him and he wondered who could have come up with such a formulation.

Talking to newsmen, he said he could not make much out of the suggestions made. Asked if he had any formula to suggest himself he said he had none as he had not been in contact with any of the parties concerned.

"It is not a metaphysical issue but one which deals with hard realities. Unless and until we know the views of the parties concerned, any exercise would be futile," he said.

Shri Shekhar answered queries of newsmen shortly before two Chief Ministers — Shri Bhairon Singh Shekhawat of Rajasthan and Shri Chimanbhai Patel of Gujarat — called on him at his residence.

Asked what would happen if the Bharatiya Janata Party (BJP) went ahead with his threat to withdraw its support to the Government, Shri Shekhar said the situation would be dealt with only when it arose.

He said the atmosphere of suspicion was not good for the country. The overall situation in the country was not, improving and the crisis was "deepening". He felt that a serious issue had been dealt with casually.

(*Hindustan Times*, October 20, 1990)

## REGIONAL ASPIRATIONS

### Promises and Precepts

Regional aspirations of the submerged groups residing in such underdeveloped areas as the eastern tribal belt call for fulfilment by appropriate measures. Equally legitimate is the demand for the application of the Sixth Schedule of the Constitution of India to some districts in the North-Eastern States such as Manipur.

### Process of Action

No tangible results.

## RESEARCH AND DEVELOPMENT

### Promises and Precepts

Our Science and Technology Policy will aim at strengthening Research and Development substantially. Indigenous technology will be developed to provide for a strong base of self-reliance and cut in import of foreign technology. It will be directed towards import substitution, development of modernised and appropriate technology and promotion of organic agricultural techniques. Non-conventional and renewable energy creation and utilisation will be one of our major objectives. The National Front has abundant faith in the capabilities of the scientific and technological community of the country, that it can shoulder these tasks magnificently.

**Process of Action**

On June 7, 1990, the Union Cabinet gave its approval for establishment of a National Council on Science and Technology to be headed by the Prime Minister.

Since 1948, there has been always a high-level apex structure with broad objectives of policy formulation and for giving direction. This, however, was discontinued in 1985 and instead a science adviser was appointed for the Prime Minister and an advisory council consisting of non-officials set-up.

With the new decision, the trend has been reversed and an apex body came into being again to advise the Union Cabinet on matters relating to science and technology.

## RIGHT TO INFORMATION

**Promises and Precepts**

*I. Open Government*

The National Front commits itself to full freedom of the media, autonomous corporations for television and radio and elimination of practices that lead to direct and indirect arm-twisting of the Press. People's right to information shall be guaranteed through Constitutional Provisions.

*II. Right to Information*

A participatory democracy requires an enlightened and informed electorate. Instead of sustaining and enlarging this basic postulate of our freedom struggle, the Rajiv Gandhi Government has choked Radio and TV with partisan and personal propaganda, prevented dissemination of facts and outraged the nation's sense of fairness.

It has also done its worst to harass and pressurise the print media from time to time. Legislative measures were attempted to gag the

Press and to end its freedom. A vigilant public opinion did not permit these measures to succeed. The Rajiv Government has increased the newsprint prices and massively burdened the economics of newspapers. The National Front commits itself to remove all such impediments. Excise duty on newsprint will be reduced and restrictions on import of newsprint removed.

One of the first acts of the National Front Government will be to liberate the electronic media from the governmental stranglehold and convert them into autonomous corporations.

The National Front Government will, by amending the Constitution, ensure the citizen's right to information. With this in mind, the Official Secrets Act will be suitably amended.

**Process of Action**

Prasar Bharati Bill has been passed.

**Public Opinion**

I. It is true, that they (National Front Government) have invited the first steps towards autonomy by introducing the Prasar Bharati Bill of 1990. But thereafter, the process stops. . . .

With the passing of the Prasar Bharati Bill and the proposed formation of a board of governors, one would have thought that the new face of broadcasting would be formulated by the new board and its director-general. And so would be the commissioning of new programmes, as envisaged by the new corporation. But it seems it is not to be.

For even before the new board is constituted Doordarshan will have decided on programmes that would be on the air for the next year or so. One begins to wonder what kind of autonomy are we talking about.

There are no easy answers. Time is running out, for Doordarshan will cease to exist after March 31, 1991. So far the board of governors is no where in sight. Even the super apex body of members of Parliament is still to be formed. Unless that happens, how will the new corporation, the Broadcasting Corporation of India function.

The only way it can function, if the board is not constituted, is to have a interim board. And that is exactly what is being planned. The interim board will be constituted by the Ministry of Information and Broadcasting and members nominated by it! Thank you Minister, Good bye autonomy.

(Ashok Raina, *Indian Express*, October 21, 1990)

II. The Prasar Bharati Act is a monument to the confusion and doublethink that have settled like a gigantic cobweb over the minds of the nation's politicians. Can'ts they ever get anything right?

In many ways, the new order amounts to old wine in new bottles. Many, many new bottles. Take, for example, the officials, including the directors-general of AIR and Doordarshan, who will run the broadcasting corporation that's supposed to kick off in April 1991. They will be deputationists from the I&B Ministry, answering, ultimately, to their minister. A far cry from any hopes that were raised of the ministry's liquidation.

In addition, the corporation's work will be subject to review and supervision by mind-boggling layers of bodies with overlapping responsibilities. The Prasar Bharati Board will have part-time members, wholetime members, ex-officio members, representatives from the I&B Ministry and "persons of eminence" to manage its affairs. A broadcasting council, nearly half of which will consist of MPs, will consider complaints against the board. A separate committee of 22 MPs will also oversee the board's functioning and report to Parliament.

This is a surefire prescription for bedlam and influence peding that will turn the corporation into another prime target for the political spoils system. And there is a final punch: the Central Government can not only demand any information from the corporation but also recommend its supersession.

Control, by any other name, is still control.

(*India Today*, October 15, 1990)

III. The Congress-I spokesperson released copies of his letter to the Information and Broadcasting Minister Shri P. Upendra, in which he had lodged "a strong protest against serious breach of faith by the National Front Government in the matter of telecasting the views of the Congress party on Mandal Commission on Doordarshan.

Shri Gadgil said an interview given by the senior leader, Shri Madhavsinh Solanki, on behalf of the party was recorded on September 21. It was telecast on October 13. This was done by ignoring two requests made by the party. The first request was made on September 25 that Shri Solanki's interview should be re-recorded to unable the party to re-state its position in view of a number of statements made by the Government after it was recorded. The second request was that this interview should be treated as cancelled, as "in view of the attitude adopted by the National Front Government in Karnataka, our party as a mark of protest does not wish to cooperate in the matter."

Shri Gadgil told Shri Upendra: "In the last few months, we have noticed both suppression and distortion of news about our party. I must warn you that if this approach and attitude continues, we will be obliged to seriously reconsider the constructive cooperation we have always offered to the National Front Government in the interest of the people of India."

Shri Gadgil told newspapers that from now onwards, Doordarshan would be "blacklisted" and would not be invited for any coverage of the party. He criticised Doordarshan for also ignoring the party president, Shri Rajiv Gandhi's "*sadbhavana yatra*", despite massive response by the people.

(*Indian Express*, October 16, 1990)

Vinod Sharma in article under the caption 'Doordarshan: Eclipse before Sunrise' observed :

On October 9, 1990 fifty-three members of Lok Sabha, in a memorandum to the Prime Minister, flayed Doordarshan's new sponsorship scheme; describing it as an attempt to "pre-empt" the Prasar Bharati Corporation. "Autonomy of the electronic media", the MPs wrote, "has to be safeguarded not only from political and bureaucratic control but also from subversion by commercial interests." One couldn't agree more with the honourable parliamentarians. Indeed, media autonomy is endangered not just by State control. Of equal concern is the possibility of backdoor invasion by big business. . . .

Open Government is more a matter of political conduct than mere legislations. Similarly, the efficacy of the new information order, inclusive of broadcasting autonomy, will depend on the quality and commitment of men in control. It is on this score that the goings-on in Doordarshan and AIR have left true lovers of free speech and right to information most apprehensive.

(*Hindustan Times*, October 21, 1990)

*Prasar Bharati*

. . . , few would maintain, . . . , that Doordarshan and AIR perform satisfactorily. Apart from the absence of any autonomy, production of programmes is unprofessional and shoddy, and the technology dated and obsolete. No attempt is made to address a particular audience or to reflect the cultural diversity and plurality of the population. What is to be done is an entirely different proposition. What is not to be done is to confine the debate on the reform of the electronic media solely to the question of autonomy and assume that once such *nirvana* is attained all other problems get solved. Autonomy or lack of it is a generic problem of all public enterprises. Even several industrial public sector units that are legally autonomous are not so in practice. But the electronic media is attended with singular constitutional and technological implications which this Bill has failed to address. All the Bill does is to hive off Doordarshan and AIR from direct government control, make it a department of state and confer autonomy through the establishment of an ostensibly autonomous corporation.

This echoes the elites' age old obsession with the BBC paradigm. Doordarshan is criticised because it is not the BBC. This obsession ignores the fact that even in the UK, the BBC model is today outdated and irrelevant. It is not longer true that the BBC sets standards for excellence. Some of the finest productions of classics and the best examples of investigative journalism have emanated from Granada, an independent television company operating under a licence. The subject of standards in broadcasting along with treatment of politically sensitive topics can easily be separated from direct government control through licensing. Once this argument is accepted there is no need for any central body on the lines of the proposed corporation. A licensing authority can safeguard public interest and at the same time permit private enterprise and community institutions the access to broadcasting.

Any intelligent attempt to reform the electronic media must take cognizance of two factors. First, the unprecedented development in communication technology that has taken place since the forties. Second, the variety of demands made on the system by a diverse public. This in turn partially arises from a political system where regional forces challenge Central authority and dictate. It is important that these otherwise fissiparrous forces are harnessed constructively and they be permitted access to the media rather than denied a voice.

And behind these two factors are two seminal issues which the Bill does not address: finance and staffing. Ultimately, the sovereign guarantee of autonomy is financial self-reliance through access to the market place rather than dependence on government largesse. And no matter how well constitutional protection afforded to the new corporation is drafted, the fact remains that its personnel will be government servants and its governors, political appointees. One is highly sceptical of whether even the much vaunted "autonomy" will amount to anything given the lack of any political consensus on this issue. Politicians love power and are exceedingly zealous about retaining it, and to expect politicians to willingly abdicate this to establish an inchoate concept such as principle, is native in the extreme.

In summary, this Bill has no meaning insofar as its central purpose — to legitimise government control over broadcasting under the rubric of "autonomy" — is misplaced and pernicious. It will only serve to set the clock back on the cause of free broadcasting and greater democratic participation in the information revolution.

(Editorial, *Business India*, September 17-30, 1990)

## RIGHT TO WORK

### Promises and Precepts

The National Front believes that every citizen has the right to productive and gainful work in order to live meaningfully and with dignity. The social and economic policy of the National Front will be geared to the realisation of the "Right to Work" as a fundamental right of the citizens of India.

We have to find productive work for the people, at wages that are commensurate with human needs and dignity. It is well within our means to generate socially productive employment on a scale necessary to convert the right to work into a reality. As a first step, new Employment Guarantee Schemes will be introduced all over the country. To realise conditions of full employment an alternative strategy of social and economic development will be followed which accords primacy to development of agriculture and allied occupations, with investment on building up infrastructure of essential physical and social services in villages and towns. Production of basic consumer goods will be reserved for cottage and small industries.

"Right to work" will be included in the Fundamental Rights guaranteed by the Constitution.

**Process of Action**

*I. Committee on Right to Work*

On October 13, 1990, Prime Minister V.P. Singh announced the formation of a committee to examine the legal, operational, organisational and financial aspects of the proposal of right to work and to give it a practical shape.

The decision to form such a committee was taken at the meeting of the National Development Council (NDC). The Council which had discussed this subject in detail had heard the opinions of different Chief Ministers on this subject. The committee will try to harmonise these opinions.

The Prime Minister has asked the committee to report within two months and after its report is received proposals on the subject will be formulated to be presented during the winter session of the Parliament. The official spokesman said that the impression created by certain reports that this proposal has been dropped or postponed was wrong.

The committee will be headed by Finance Minister Madhu Dandavate and have Chief Ministers of Assam, Bihar, Gujarat, Maharashtra, Orissa, Rajasthan, Tamil Nadu and West Bengal as members. Dr. A. Vaidyanathan and Shri L. C. Jain members of the Planning Commission will also be members of the Committee. Shri Jain will act as Member-Secretary of the Committee and Secretary Finance will be permanent invitee to the committee to assist it in its deliberations.

The committee will examine all aspects of the scheme for right to work and suggest a legal, financial and administrative set up as well as its phasing in its report. It will also suggest means for resource mobilisation and role of State Governments and local bodies.

*II. Three Million More Jobs Planned*

On September 29, 1990 the Government announced a major programme to facilitate generation of additional three million jobs for educated unemployed in the private sector by 1994-95.

The proposed plan of action seeks to create three million additional jobs — 0.5 million for graduates and 2.5 million for non-graduates — and these employment opportunities have to be created outside the Government sector which is already heavily overburdened, the spokesman said.

A high-level committee of officials is being set-up to formulate details of the action plan, the spokesman said.

The spokesman indicated that economic policies would be reformulated in such a manner that they are conducive to employment creation in the private sector.

The National Sample Survey (NSS) data have projected the total number of educated unemployed in the country (matriculation and above) at about five million. The Government's calculations appear to be that if three million additional jobs are to be provided in the next five years, there would be a backlog of two million at the end of 1994-95. The number of unemployed graduates is estimated by the NSS survey at 1.5 million. The spokesman described the action plan as a serious attempt by the Government to tackle the problem of educational unemployed.

Explaining the details of the action plan, the spokesman said it proposed reformulation of economic strategies to encourage use of more labour and less capital in the private sector, specific time-bound action plans for increasing employment opportunities through vocational training and creation of self-employment opportunities.

He said in solving the problem of educated unemployed, first it is necessary to train them through vocational education, to acquire skills in traces or professions which would make them employable in the private sector where there is excess demand and employment opportunities exist.

Secondly, it is essential to create more opportunities for self-employed among the educated, by using financial institutions to provide the requisite support in terms of modest capital needs and using downstream self-employment opportunities created by the Government sector, particularly in service and distribution activities. Thirdly, it is imperative that they are conducive to employment creation in the private sector. "Our experience in the recent past has been just the opposite where incentives and disincentives implicit in the policy regime encourage the use of capital and discourage use of labour", the spokesman said.

He said specific, time-bound action plans have been proposed for increasing employment opportunities in the private sector through vocational training.

Details of the training and employment generation programme are as follows:

| | Additional | Trainees | Employment generation potential |
|---|---|---|---|
| ITIs | 1993-94 | 50,000 | |
| Apprenticeship | 1994-95 | 1,00,000 | 1,50,000 |
| Polytechnics | 1993-94 | 20,000 | |
| | 1994-95 | 40,000 | 60,000 |
| Computer | H. level | 1,25,000 | |
| Professionals | L. level | 5,00,000 | 6,25,000 |
| Consumer and electronics | technicians | 50,000 | |
| Service centre | Helpers | 1,25,000 | 1,75,000 |
| SEEUY | 2.5 lakh per year for 4-year | | 10,00,000 |
| Micro enterprises | -do- | | 10,00,000 |
| Public sector 10,000 initially with 10 per cent growth | | | |
| | | | 15,000 |
| Voluntary women's organisations | 5,000 per year for 4 years | | 20,000 |
| | | | 30,45,000 |

Broad break-up: Graduate — 0.5 million
Non-graduate — 2.5 million

## Public Opinion

### *I. Where are the Jobs?*

Abishek Manu Singhvi, has in an article has posed this question: Where are the jobs? He has elaborated the theme as, "Indians, as a nation, seem to be particularly mesmerised by the hypnotic effect of words and abstractions. Rightly did Rudyard Kipling say: "Words and phrases are, of course, the most powerful drugs used by mankind:. In the present situation of our country, the guarantee of the Right to Work is one such addictive phrase fashioned by a native or a knavish thought process. The rousing and ringing proclamation of a proposed constitutional Right to Work is yet another piece of populism rather than a concrete blueprint to work out an employment generation programme, with cold hard statistics. It is conveniently digressive, escapist and tangential, if not quite flippant and comic. The mere enactment of the constitutional right to work or eat is not likely to provide work or food for anyone, except perhaps for the draftsman and the politician who incorporate it in the Constitution. Obviously, fair words do not fill the belly. Promising the right to work is of course easy. Performing on that promise is extremely difficult. Our path is already strewn with unfulfilled promises. So why not make one more, without giving any real and substantial thought to the provision of full employment by comprehensive economic policies, by innovative employment generation schemes, by well conceived agricultural programmes, by grassroots provision of job opportunities, by wise governance, by the efficient organisation of the economic system and by a whole host of other similar concrete, pragmatic and result-oriented methods and techniques? Clearly, the expansive promise of the constitutional Right to Work is to offer a simplistic and catchy legal or constitutional panacea without the economic, financial, agricultural and industrial wherewithal. That is the stuff of which our populist politics is made.

*Distant Fantasy*

The concept of a universally available constitutional right to work is a distant fantasy and an empty shibboleth. Whether one is a socialist or a capitalist, a mixed economist or a mixed up politician, there is no gainsaying the fact that a right, by definition, has to be economically and socially viable and legally enforceable. The so-called "Right to Work" would most certainly, neither be viable nor enforceable without a comprehensive plan and massive inputs. Even a paper plan would not do because we just cannot afford it. Where are the resources? Even if the Finance Minister resorted to fifty or hundred times the present level of deficit financing and printed currency notes without any fiscal inhibitions, we cannot give jobs to all the fifty to hundred million unemployed and the underemployed in our country.

A single job requires roughly US $ 1,275 (Rs. 21,812.50) per year. At that rate and at the conservative estimate of 50 million unemployed in the country, the Government of India has to dole out $ 53,750 million which is equivalent to the astronomical figure of Rs. 9,13,750 million. Do we have that kind of money to spare? Imagine an unemployed Indian citizen obtaining a mandamus from a court of law to give him a job because of the guarantee of the Right to Work and discovering that both the right and the remedy amount to nothing but a pyrrhic paper consolation. In the result, we would have nothing but futile writs issued by courts, perhaps fifty million pointless contempt proceedings bringing the whole legal system into disrepute and wholesale frustration and disillusionment all around. A more scatter-brained promise has yet to see the light of the day.

*Dole of Money*

Would the Right to Work be satisfied and effectuated simply by providing a dole of money? Would a petition claiming money in lieu of work be maintainable? Would mere economic assistance qualify as actual, honourable work? Do we have the national resources, the billions and trillions of rupees to provide dole to our 50 million (minimum) unemployed? Moreover, is it desirable to introduce or extend the concept of dole into Indian society, when nations which have had it for years have rejected it or are struggling to escape from its crippling strangle-hold? What would happen to the employer's right to terminate the services of an errant employee? For then the Right to Work is bound to be affected. How shall we cope with collective bargaining and the Right to Work at the same time? Have we identified and analysed these issues and their ramifications?

The Right to Work is a powerful combination of words, stirring up heroic images of a triumphant struggle for human dignity. But the stark reality is that the Indian economy and the powers that be are wholly unequal to the task of realising and fulfilling that right as of today. That is why a plea for sanity and moderation has to be entered lest words of constitutional significance are used as masks for political loose talk or meaningless bravado."

(*Hindustan Times*, September 30, 1990)

*II. The Right to What?*

No one disputes the fact that the Central Government simply does not have the resources to underwrite a constitutional guarantee to the right to work. It has been reliably estimated that Rs. 10,000 crore, at the least, will be required to fund a country-wide employment guarantee programme on the lines of Maharashtra's Employment Guarantee

Scheme. The Central Government has taken no steps in the last ten months to show that resources of this dimension can indeed be raised either by fresh taxes or by drastic budget reallocations. It has not had the political will, as the previous government did not either, to trim the fat from other heads of expenditure or cut subsidies in order to keep its deficits within manageable limits. No substantial enhancement of the Jawahar Rozgar Yojana has taken place (an anti-poverty programme which does not guarantee work and wages on demand but provides a small safety net for some of the poor).

Undeterred by such realities, the Government goes on being profligate in its promises about the Right to Work. . . .

The latest meeting of the National Development Council has come in very handy. The collective wisdom of all the Chief Ministers assembled there can now be blamed for the decision to postpone indefinitely a right to work policy (and presumably a constitutional amendment). A committee consisting of representatives of the Central and State Governments and the Planning Commission is to be appointed to prepare a "practical formula" for implementation of the Right to Work. The NDC felt resources and work potential should be examined "carefully". This is sensible. The country must be spared any more half-baked policies on the ground that the manifesto has to be lived up to. Rather caution than another Himalayan blunder. Better a practical formula based on consensus than the partisan pursuit of utopian dreams.

But the Janata Dal and the Prime Minister cannot get off so lightly. In recent days two new announcements have been made: the creation of three million additional jobs by 1995 (against the current unemployment figure of 18 million); a proposal to raise the annual growth rate of employment to thre per cent during the Eighth Plan (against two per cent during the last decade). The Government must set out in a white paper or otherwise what direction it would like to give its employment policy. The "Right to Work" means all things to all people. It could mean bigger, better anti-poverty programmes or the pursuit of a full employment economic strategy, enlarging the public sector or boosting the private sector. Is the guarantee to be for jobs commensurate with one's skill and education or for any kind of job? In perpetuity or for a limited number of days in the year? What does the Government have in mind? In the last ten months, has it developed any serious thoughts on these questions.

(Editorial, *Indian Express*, October 15, 1990)

## RURAL ECONOMY

### Promises and Precepts

The National Front will evolve a set of long overdue policies for the benefit of the neglected farming community and the rural society. Not less than 50 per cent of the investible resources will be deployed for the development of rural economy. Farmers will be assured of guaranteed remunerative prices for their produce, a countrywide network of godowns and warehouses, remission of debts, provision of cheap credit, removal of unreasonable restrictions on movement of agricultural produce, crop insurance, security in land-holding and strict implementation of land reforms and improved access to water resources.

### Process of Action

The Planning Commission has taken necessary steps and has issued guidelines for stepping up outlays on agriculture and allied sectors. The Union Budget for 1990-91 has provided for this. Other budgetary measures to help the rural sector include allocation of Rs. 4,000 crore towards fertilizer subsidy; concessional import duty on specified pesticides; removal of excise duty on refined rapeseed/mustard seed oil; and Rs 1,000 crore for implementing the debt relief scheme for small farmers, artisans and weavers.

*Debt Relief Scheme/Loan Waiver Scheme*

The framework for the debt relief scheme has been announced.

Farmers who had taken loans for agriculture and related activities, landless farm labourers, artisans and weavers who had taken loans for vocational requirements will be covered under the scheme. The relief would cover all overdues on short term and other term loans advanced by public sector banks, regional rural banks, as on October 2, 1989. Once the eligibility of the borrowers for debt relief is established, the waiver of the principal and interest amounts would be allowed up to a limit of Rs. 10,000. This measure is likely to cost the Centre and the State about Rs. 3,000 crore.

**Public Opinion**

Shri Chavan, in the Parliament on August 7, 1990 described the loan waiver scheme as a big fraud played upon the people of this country by the National Front. In the first instance, the Government was to waive off Rs. 10,000 loan, but now the Finance Minister was saying that only Rs. 4,400 could be waived off. He wondered if this scheme could ever be implemented.

(*Indian Express*, August 8, 1990)

The decision to write off loans of ruralites up to Rs. 10,000 inevitably smacks of political motivation. There used to be quite a hue and cry against the loan meals when they were held during the preceding regime. The wholesale writing off of loans is ostensibly the same thing, in another shape, and even worse. One would strongly advocate the writing off of the loan of a person who has, because of circumstances beyond his control, become incapable of repaying the loan. In such cases, the loan must be written off. All indigents, whether in rural areas or in urban sectors, deserve to receive this treatment equally. But there cannot be any justification for wholesale writing off of all loans up to Rs. 10,000 as appears to have been decided in the present dispensation. And what justification can there be for writing off Rs. 10,000 part of a bigger loan that has been given to a ruralite? This decision of the government is coming in for severe criticism. It tends to undermine the credibility of the banking system itself. What justification can the banks put forth for writing off the loans where they are repayable? And, if the government comes to their rescue by offering them subsidies, who eventually pays for these subsidies? It is the tax-payer's money, say the critics, which the government will be passing on as subsidy to the banks for enabling them to write off the loans. This criticism is gathering momentum and arbitrariness of the executive in taking a decision of this nature will surely be challengeable.

(*Competition Success Review*, Special Number, 1990)

## SALES TAX

**Promises and Precepts**

The present system of Sales Tax will be rationalised.

### Process of Action

No tangible results.

## SCHEDULED CASTES, SCHEDULED TRIBES AND OTHER BACKWARD CLASSES

### Promises and Precepts

The National Front is committed to removal of social inequality in all forms.

Implementation of reservation policy will be made effective in government, public and private sector industrial undertakings, banking institutions, etc., by resorting to special recruitment drives so as to fulfil their quotas within the shortest possible time.

The Scheduled Castes and Scheduled Tribes Commission will be armed with statutory powers.

Preferential opportunities and concessions will be ensured to scheduled castes, even after they embrace Buddhism, in view of the fact that they continue to suffer from social disability.

Special courts will be constituted to try cases concerning atrocities against scheduled castes and scheduled tribes and the violation of "Protection of Civil Rights Act".

Steps shall be taken to fight all vestiges of untouchability and social disabilities. Propagation of untouchability shall be severely dealt with.

The tribals' interests will be fully protected and various hardships and evictions, which they face owing to ill-conceived forest laws and arbitrary actions of forest officials, will be removed. Their customary laws will be respected and observed. Wherever tribal lands have been occupied by others, without survey operations being held, these will be restored after conducting survey operations. Their special needs will be attended to in the formulations and execution of forest policies and they will be made active participants in the process of massive afforestation.

The socially and educationally backward classes will be given special opportunities and substantial reservations in employment, education and public offices.

The recommendations of the Mandal Commission will be implemented expeditiously.

**Process of Action**

*1990-91 Social Justice Year*

Prime Minister V.P. Singh, while paying his tribute to Dr. Babasaheb Bhimarao Ramji Ambedkar on April 14, 1990 declared the year 1990-91 a year of social justice.

(*Hindustan Times*, April 15, 1990)

*Other Steps*

The very first legislation passed in Parliament after the new Government took over extended reservation for scheduled castes and scheduled tribes in the Lok Sabha and the State Assemblies for another 10 years.

The Scheduled Castes and Scheduled Tribes (Prevention of Atrocities) Act, 1989 came into force from 30th January, 1990. This Act identifies types of atrocities and provides for effective machinery, such as special courts and special prosecutors, to quickly deal with the cases. It also details stringent punishment of the guilty. Some of the State Governments have set up special courts. The States which have not taken action have been asked to set up such courts in a month's time.

Action is being taken to restore land rights to the scheduled castes and scheduled tribes who had been divested of them. Backlog of vacancies reserved for SCs and STs in government are to be filled up at the earliest.

Legislation to ensure round-the-year work for agricultural labourers, higher subsidy for SC families under the Integrated Rural Development Programme, extension of SC benefits to neo-Buddhists are some of the other steps taken to improve the economic status of these people who had been victims of social oppression for a number of years.

Conferring of Bharat Ratna on Dr. Ambedkar and the unveiling of his portrait in the Central Hall of Parliament reflects the determination of the Government to fulfil the yearnings of the toiling masses.

*SC and ST Facilities for Neo-Buddhists*

Parliamentary approval was given for extending the facilities provided to scheduled castes and scheduled tribes to neo-Buddhists with the Lok Sabha approving the Constitution Amendment Bill on May 29, 1990.

The Bill had been earlier approved by the Rajya Sabha. Replying to the discussion Minister for Labour and Welfare Ram Vilas Paswan announced that the Government would soon convene an all-party meeting to evolve a consensus for the extension of the facilities provided to scheduled castes to other religious minorities also.

The Minister said that the National Front Government did not have any "negative attitude" and it would abide by the consensus reached at a meeting of all the parties. He said that the Centre has received a large number of representation for inclusion of various tribes in the scheduled tribes category.

Shri Paswan said that the representation was under study and the Government would soon come out with a comprehensive Bill on the subject. He said that efforts should be made to create awareness among the scheduled castes and scheduled tribes to enable them to become self-reliant. For this there was need to educate them. He claimed that the recruitment drive for scheduled caste and scheduled tribe was going on and they have decided to organise training programme of technical education so that they could acquire necessary skills to qualify for the jobs.

(*Hindustan Times*, May 30, 1990)

*SC and ST Panel Powers*

Shri Ram Dhan, MP, Chairman, National Commission for scheduled castes and scheduled tribes, said on October 17, 1990 that this commission was without any "teeth" and it appeared that the Welfare Ministry wanted to treat the commission as its appendage "which is clearly not acceptable to the commission as well as Parliament".

He said there were more than 5,000 petitions relating to atrocities, service matters and other grievances received at commission. Unfortunately, the commission was not in a position to deal with these petitions at present as they fell beyond the existing jurisdiction of the commission.

The Dalits and other disadvantaged groups of the society were earnestly looking towards the Prime Minister for ending the present stalemate immediately to render justice to the interests of the scheduled castes and scheduled tribes.

Shri Ram Dhan said there were repeated announcements by the

Ministry that the commission had been vested with considerable powers. This aroused the hopes of the SCs and the STs but now they appear to feel that the commission was not able to deliver goods.

The reality was that though Parliament amended Article 338 of the Constitution in May last and the President gave his assent to the Bill on June 7, 1990, yet it had not been put into effect so far. Consequently, the commission continued to be without any teeth and was merely functioning as a body to conduct studies — a role to which it was relegated in September, 1987".

*Statement of the Prime Minister on Second Backward Classes Commission, August 7, 1990*

The following is the text of the *suo motu* statement of Prime Minister in the Lok Sabha on decisions on the Mandal Commission Report:

> I am happy today to announce in this august House a momentous decision of social justice that my Government has taken regarding the Socially and Educationally Backward Classes on the basis of the Report of the Mandal Commission.
>
> Hon'ble Members are aware that the Constitution which we gave to ourselves 40 years back envisages that Socially and Educationally Backward Classes (SEBCs) be identified, their difficulties removed and their conditions improved in terms of Article 340(1) read with Article 15(4) as well as Article 16(4). It is a negation of the basic structure of our Constitution that till now this requirement was not fulfilled.
>
> The Second Backward Classes Commission under the Chairmanship of the late Shri B.P. Mandal which was appointed on 1st July, 1979 submitted its report on 31st December 1980. In accordance with our commitment before the people we included this in our Action Plan. After examining various aspects of it, I am glad to announce that my Government has taken the following decisions on the Commission's Report:
>
> (i) In order to avail ourselves of the benefit of the long experience of a number of States in preparing lists of Socially and Educationally Backward Classes (SEBCs) and in order to ensure harmonious and quick implementation, we have decided to adopt in the first phase the castes common to both

the Mandal list as well as the State Lists.

(ii) The percentage of reservation for the Socially and Educationally Backward Classes (SEBCs) will be 27.

(iii) This reservation will be applicable to services under the Government of India and Public Undertakings.

Hon'ble Members are aware that on 14 April, 1990 at the official function organised to celebrate the birthday of Bharat Ratna Baba Saheb Dr. B.R. Ambedkar at the Ambedkar Stadium, I announced the commencement of the Ambedkar Centenary Year and designated it as the Year of Social Justice. We have taken a number of measures of social justice pertaining to the scheduled castes and scheduled tribes and other weaker sections like removal of injustice done to neo-Buddhists vesting of constitutional status and substantial powers to the National Commission for scheduled castes and scheduled tribes, according due but long delayed honours to Dr. Ambedkar, and so on. The present decisions are in the same line and belong to the tradition of this Government's dedication to the cause of the scheduled castes, scheduled tribes, socially and educationally backward classes and other weaker sections.

*Office Memorandum on Recommendations of the Second Backward Classes Commission (Mandal Report): Reservation for Socially and Educationally Backward Classes in Services under the Government of India*

In a multiple undulating society like ours, early achievement of the objective of social justice as enshrined in the Constitution is a must. The Second Backward Classes Commission called the Mandal Commission was established by the then Government with this purpose in view, which submitted its report to the Government of India on December 31, 1980.

2. Government have carefully considered the report and the recommendations of the Commission in the present context regarding the benefits to be extended to the socially and educationally backward classes as opined by the Commission and are of the clear view that at the outset certain weightage has to be provided to such classes in the services of the Union and their public undertakings. Accordingly orders are issued as follows:

(i) Twenty-seven per cent of the vacancies in civil posts and services under the Government of India shall be reserved for SEBCs.

(ii) The aforesaid reservation shall apply to vacancies to be filled by direct recruitment. Detailed instructions relating to the procedure to be followed for enforcing reservation will be issued separately.

(iii) Candidates belonging to SEBCs recruited on the basis of merit in an open competition on the same standards prescribed for the general candidates shall not be adjusted against the reservation quota of twenty-seven per cent.

(iv) The SEBCs would comprise in the first phase the castes and communities which are common to both the list in the report of the Mandal Commission and the State Government's list A.

(v) The aforesaid reservation shall take effect from August 7, 1990. However, this will not apply to vacancies where the recruitment process has already been initiated prior to the issue of these orders.

3. Similar instructions in respect of public sector undertakings and financial institutions including public sector banks will be issued by the Department of Public Enterprises and Ministry of Finance respectively.

**Public Opinion**

*UK Press*

The unanimous verdict of the British Press on the current controversy over the Mandal Commission is that Shri V.P. Singh is playing a vote game which is bound to split India.

By far the most sensible article has come from Shri Bernard Levin, eminent commentator, in the *Times*. The Mandal report, he writes in a remarkable assessment of the situation, was "sensibly shelved by the then Government as partly dangerous, partly unworkable and partly lunatic. All sensible folk assumed it would never be heard again. Nor was it, until the beleaguered V. P. Singh, shaky Prime Minister of an almost equally shaky coalition, remembered the Mandal report and concluded that it held great promise of electoral support".

However, Shri Levin is critical that successive Indian Governments failed to break the hideous chains of caste, which condemn hundreds of million of people to the worst jobs, the worst dwellings, the worst contempt which is the greatest stain on India's democracy. Even Mahatma Gandhi with his huge influence, could not shake the abominable ladder. Much of the opposition comes from the higher castes. They are demonstrating not at the obviously disastrous effects of such a policy, let alone at the centuries-old injustice of the caste system itself, but in defence of their privileged position, put a risk if the policy is implemented. There is, of course, a less selfish aspect to the upheaval.

If the Mandal plan goes through, it will push India a long way towards total catastrophe. The affections of the backward and scheduled castes include their lack of educational opportunities. Just imagine what the Indian governmental machine would be like after a few years of being run by people chosen not because they are the best people to run it but because they were born in humble circumstances. He goes further. In his view, the implementation of the Mandal proposals will mean a much greater disaster than the wreckings of the machinery of the Government.

He writes: "What the scheme offers is what has come to be called affirmative action, in its most extreme form. The principle is familiar to us from the world of race relations. It makes no bones about giving advantages to minority groups.

Like most such matters, this approach has gone farthest in the United States, where it has been a disastrous monument to misplaced generosity. In the US and Britain, the authorities have ignored the inevitable resentment of those, no less deserving, who are denied the special favours. They have built psychological ghettos of jobs, schools and housing. In India, of all nations, the Government proposes to institute, in its most extravagant form and amid the fiercest opposition, this discredited and dangerous system, for no more worthy purpose than to cling to political power. The backward castes are a vote bank, and Shri V.P. Singh is determined to draw upon it even if it should split the country irreparably.

Describing the Mandal report as 'crazy', Shri Levin says that if it is pushed through its only effect will be greater determination on the part of the higher castes to keep the barriers up, more confused anger on the part of those it seeks to help, obstacles in the path of real reconciliation, more neglect of India's real problems, and more flames amid which more young people will die in agony on the pavements of Delhi.

The *Financial Times* has been first to report the electoral design behind Shri V.P. Singh's determination to go ahead with the Mandal report. The *Independent* says that few Indian politicians disagree with the idea of improving the lot of India's wretched classes, but many distrust the Prime Minister's timing.

(*Hindustan Times*, October 15, 1990)

**General Observations**

The reservations are in pursuance of the recommendations of the Second Backward Classes Commission under the chairmanship of the late Shri B.P. Mandal, which was appointed on January 1, 1979. The Commission submitted its report on December 31, 1980.

The announcement raises to 49.5 per cent reservation of jobs for various classes, since there is already a reservation of 15 per cent for the scheduled castes and 7.5 per cent for the scheduled tribes. This is keeping with a Supreme Court Directive in 1980 not to exceed the reservation by 50 per cent.

All the political parties in the country are for special measures for the advancement of the socially and educationally backward classes, "but" to quote Nitish Chakravarty, "the Government's lack of fineness in dealing with so emotive an issue has not only given the Opposition Congress (I) a godsend to harass the Prime Minister but strained the National Front's relations with the friendly parties who feel let down at not being consulted." He also observed, "Even those who do not question the Prime Minister's motives for invoking the Mandal formula find it hard to defend the raking up of the controversy at a time when the Government is shaking at the foundations over issues such as Punjab, Kashmir and Assam. They take it as one more instance of V.P. Singh's lack of dexterity in the game of politics. Anyone well-versed in the art of politics would have tried to find out why the Congress (I) had sat on the Mandal report for 10 years. If it was the best route to the OBCs' hearts, neither Indira Gandhi nor Rajiv Gandhi would have allowed the report to gather dust. They must have been advised that the Frankenstein was best left to itself." . . .

There has never been anything like it. The nation is still reeling in horror at the spate of self-immolations by young students protesting against the Mandal report. Certainly it would appear that the indifferent method of the Government's handling the students' agitation had a great deal to do with the eruption of the particular method of protest.

The statements of a few Cabinet Ministers seems to have added fuel to the fire.

It is really very shocking that all the major political parties remained by and large, silent to the plight of the students.

*Vacancies in the Central Government and Implications of Reservations*

| | 1985 | 1986 | 1987 | 1988 |
|---|---|---|---|---|
| Graduate and post-graduates registered at employment exchanges | 24 lakh | 28.61 lakh | 28.15 lakh | 28.67 lakh |
| Total vacancies | 226,781 | 220,788 | 221,470 | 204,288 |
| General categories | 114,525 | 111,498 | 111,843 | 103,166 |
| Scheduled castes/ scheduled tribes | 51,025 | 49,677 | 49,830 | 45,964 |
| Other Backward castes (If Mandal Commission was implemented) | 61,231 | 59,613 | 59,797 | 55,158 |

## SOCIAL TASKS

*See*

Art and Culture
Education
Ex-servicemen
Fishermen
Health and Family Welfare
Housing as a Right
Language Policy
Old and the Handicapped
Scheduled Castes, Scheduled Tribes and Other Backward Classes
Women: Equal Status for Women
Youth

## UNION-STATE RELATIONS

### Promises and Precepts

#### *I. True Federalism*

The National Front is committed to true federalism, and will reverse the over-centralisation brought about by the ruling party. Not only will the States benefit by decentralisation of powers from the Centre, but there will be a corresponding and simultaneous devolution of power to the districts, the taluks, tahsils, the mandals and the Panchayats, on the basis of a national consensus.

*II. Union-State Relations*

We firmly believe that genuine federalism alone can broaden and deepen the bonds of unity and integrity of our great nation. The National Front believes that the strengthening of the States need not be at the expense of the Union and will, on the other hand, enable the Union to discharge its responsibilities more effectively.

The States ought to enjoy genuine autonomy — political, legislative, economic, fiscal and administrative — without submitting themselves to the indignity of becoming supplicants before the Centre, with a begging bowl.

Successive attempts have been made by the Union Government, under Rajiv Gandhi, to encroach upon the autonomy of the States.

The National Front will undertake a comprehensive review of Union-State relations, in consultation with all Chief Ministers and having regard to the reports to the Commissions and Committees on the subject and the representations made to them by the States and political parties. On this basis, it will strengthen the federal nature of the Indian polity so as to make it responsive to the aspirations of the people living in various States.

The National Front is Committed to:

* establish an Inter-State Council under Article 263 of the Constitution;
* activate the National Development Council in order to achieve and maintain a national consensus on all issues relating to planning and development. The Planning Commission will be given a constitutional status and will function as an executive arm of the National Development Council;
* not to misuse for political purposes, Article 356 relating to the dismissal of State Governments. Legislative Assemblies — not Raj Bhavans — will be the forum for testing the strength of the duly elected Ministries in States;
* ensure that Governors are not used as agents of the party in power

in the Centre. The National Front will ensure constitutional accountability of the Governor by bringing in necessary amendments to the Constitution. The role, powers and functions of the Governors, as also whether any alternative arrangements can be made, will be examined; and

* to devolve adequate financial and administrative powers to States to enable them to discharge their responsibilities to the people.

**Process of Action**

The first meeting of the Inter-State Council was held on October 10, 1990. The main subjects discussed were: Sarkaria Commission recommendations, inter-State consignment tax, transfer of excise duty on man-made fibres to the fibre-yarn stage and setting up special courts to deal with narcotic and psychotrophic related economic offences.

The National Development Council (NDC), discussed on October 10, 1990, the modification needed in the Gadgil formula of Central Assistance to States and issues relating to the implementation of the Right to Work.

## WATER MANAGEMENT

**Promises and Precepts**

The National Front firmly believes that the stability of our national life is totally linked to the stability of our water system. Primary importance will be given to ensuring long term water stability through (1) harvesting rain water in catchment areas, thereby effectively controlling floods and restoring the perennial character of Indian rivers and augmenting groundwater recharge, (2) conserving water use in both agriculture and industry, and (3) strict protection of water-system from pollution by industry, civic authorities, etc.

The irrigation policies of the National Front Government will be based on a rational water-management approach, of developing tiny water-sheds and the sub-basins, fulfilling the needs of the local population, while effectively controlling floods and also ensuring the riparian rights of the downstream people. Priority in irrigation will be given to minor and medium projects.

Formation of a national grid to optimise utilisation of water resources will be pursued.

The potential of river Brahmaputra shall be harnessed through long term measures to combat floods and generate power.

The National Front Government will find an expeditious solution to Inter-State water disputes in a fair and equitable manner.

**Process of Action**

No tangible results.

## WOMEN

**Promises and Precepts**

*I. Equal Status for Women*

Women, constituting half the population, shall be enabled to live with self-respect and free from oppression and indignity. The basis for the social policy of the National Front shall be to guarantee women equality with men before law and to discourage and ultimately eliminate all those practices which militate against social equality of the sexes. It will make India a signatory to the U.N. Convention on Women's Rights and ensure that its policies and programmes for women flow from its charter.

A statutory All India Commission on Women will be appointed to monitor and accelerate the process of equal representation for women, to enforce all legislation for women's rights, including labour laws, and to check discrimination in all spheres.

The National Front will take all steps to enable women to fully participate in the development process. It will plan for the creation of jobs on a massive scale for women, particularly in the agrarian sector through agro-industries. Special vocational training institutions shall be set up for women to encourage self-employment, as well as to increase their eligibility for recruitment in industrial enterprises and offices. There will be 30 per cent reservation for women in government jobs, with preference to the destitute, widowed, divorced, deserted and to women heads of households. The private sector will be encouraged to employ more women. The principle of equal pay for equal or similar work will be upheld. Funds for special employment generating sectors more conductive to women's employment shall be specially earmarked and augmented.

A Maternity Fund will be created to benefit needy pregnant women, including the self-employed for the first two deliveries. Maternity health and child care will be included in the minimum needs programme.

There will be special emphasis on women's education.

The National Front commits to provide public latrines (*Sulabh Sauchalayas*) for the use of women in all villages in the next five years. Smokeless *Chulhas* will be subsidised and made available on a large scale to reduce drudging of women in the kitchens.

A review will be undertaken of all social legislation concerning marriage, divorce, maintenance, custody, adoption, inheritance, etc., in consultation with women's organisations and all concerned communities, enact new legislation to give women equal rights in all these matters. Strict punishment will be given to those who violate laws meant to protect women's rights and abate crimes like *Sati* or dowry murders. All forms of harassment and violence against women will be strictly punished.

Suitable enactments will be undertaken to confer equal rights for women in the parental properties.

The National Front believes that no women should go shelterless. Women-headed households and destitute women shall be given priority in allotment of housing loans. Housing sites allotted by the Government will be jointly registered in the name of husband and wife. Land distributed under land reforms schemes will be jointly registered. More shelter homes will be opened for destitute women and they shall be given vocational training and rehabilitated. More women's hostels with provision to accommodate children, will be provided.

Depiction of women in any form of obscenity and indignity will be banned through stringent legislation. Participation of women's organisations to monitor this will be sought. Media will be used to project more positive image of women.

### *II. Women's Participation*

Our success in national reconstruction will depend on the equal participation and involvement of women. The front will, therefore, accordingly, give special attention to ensure this.

**Process of Action**

*I. Special Role for Women*

According to the approach paper to the Eighth Plan, women will be accorded a special role in the scheme of decentralised are a planning and mobilisation of local skills and resources.

The status of women as producers of goods and services and as rightful claimants of social security will be explicitly recognised and maximum resources will be directed towards releasing the productive and creative energies of rural women so that they become equal partners in the socio-cultural transformation of the society.

Indiscriminate use of science and technology has in many cases added to the difficulties of women in protecting their jobs and incomes. The first step was a recognition of the dignity of women's work and a proper understanding of its dimensions and contribution in the Indian context, the approach paper says.

The paper has identified positive thrust areas during the Plan period including determined steps for identification of women workers and their registration.

The basic approach would be to empower women by raising their status and bring them into the mainstream of national development not as mere beneficiaries but as contributors and partakers along with men.

Existing lacunae in conceptual frame and database referred to earlier will be corrected and applied research encouraged for this purpose.

Constraints and hurdles will be removed in order to expand their access to an control over resources, through legal and administrative action.

The approach paper says the criteria and processes for determination of wages and social security will be reviewed and rationalised to provide recognition and equitable return for women's work of all kinds.

Women who have been victims of wanton destruction of their fragile survival systems for food, fodder, fuel, water and raw material will be encouraged to get organised so as to play a leadership role in ecological regeneration.

They will be encouraged to mobilise themselves to join cooperative trade unions, associations and other democratic organisations with a view to realising their full potential for development.

Recognising the fact that women constitute half the population and are critical to the production and social processes of the economy, the approach paper says that their contribution and role in the family as well as in economic development and social transformation are pivotal. It notes that women have been managing and supporting the survival systems, particularly in the case of the poor households constituting about 30 per cent of the population. The programme for alleviation of poverty should have a strong focus on development of women, the paper says.

(*Hindustan Times*, May 27, 1990)

*II. Women's Panel Bill*

The Lok Sabha passed without a dissenting voice the Bill to constitute a National Commission for Women amidst all round jubilation among every section of the House, particularly for the ten women members from six parties who were present at the time of final voting late in the evening of August 9, 1990.

While Shri Ram Vilas Paswan, Minister of Welfare carried the entire House with him by promising incorporation of various amendments moved by Members in the rules that would be framed, his junior colleague Smt. Usha Sinha . . . , described the Bill as historic. No member moved any amendment.

The role of the women members of the House cutting across party lines in getting the Bill passed on August 9, 1990 itself was one of the highlights of the long debate, when at one stage they appealed with folded hands to the Congress-I Member P.J. Kurien not to press for adjournment of the House after six p.m. . . . Shri Kurien relented. A Congress-I member Mrs Jamuna too had pleaded with Shri Kurien to let the debate continue.

The women members present at the time of voting were Smt. Geeta Mukherjee of the CPI, Mrs Vasundhara Raje, Smt. Jawantiben Mehta and Smt. Sumitra Mahajan of the BJP, Smt. Malini Bhattacharya and Smt. Suasini Ali of the CPI-M, Smt. Mayavati of the Bahujan Samaj Party, and Smt. Jamuna of the Congress-I, besides Smt. Usha Sinha.

**Public Opinion**

Under its editorial 'Watchdog or lapdog', dated August 8, 1990, the *Hindustan Times* made these observations:

"It is too early to evaluate the National Commission for Women Bill (NCW) passed by the Lok Sabha. For, while there are still some lacunae in it, what is important to know is how will its provisions be implemented. One can, at this state, only agree with Prime Minister V.P. Singh that the NCW is just the first step towards making the constitutional guarantee of equality for women a reality. However, the fact that the Lok Sabha which enthusiastically and unanimously passed this Bill has much fewer women members than the previous one may cause some cynicism as to how far could the National Front Government be persuaded in implementing this assurance.

The NCW is supposed to be a watchdog body. While it will be a statutory body and should be able to investigate and do research on issues of concern to women, particularly as it has the power to set up committees to do so, the method of nomination of members to the apex body and their continuation makes them dependent on the government's goodwill. In a situation where the government is the major violator of the constitutional guarantees and of other laws that have been made for the benefit of women, how can such a commission be fearless in indicting the government?

However, on the plus side, as Welfare Minister Ram Vilas Paswan has pointed out, the NCW would enjoy all the powers under the Commission of Inquiry Act. It can investigate all complaints including those relating to atrocities against women. While it would not have penal powers, an FIR could be lodged on the basis of its inquiry report. It could *suo motu* take notice of matters relating to infringement of women's rights, non-implementation of laws and non-compliance of policy decisions relating to the welfare of women. It could also summon witnesses and call for information. Any failure to comply could lead to contempt proceedings in a civil court. It is to be seen if Shri Paswan will live up to his promise to incorporate some of the amendments suggested in the rules."

(*Hindustan Times*, August 8, 1990)

*NCW: A Mere Token*

Despite vociferous protests by several women organisations on the proposed National Commission on Women (NCW), Doordarshan lauded its establishment emphasising that the NCW represented a consensus of the views of several women's organisations.

The NCW will be a statutory body to investigate the deprivation of women's rights, the non-implementation and review of laws affecting women, and the inspection of remand homes and the housing of female prisoners. But it falls short on two vital aspects — the commission has only limited powers and an inadequate staff to fulfil these onerous obligations, and secondly, it lacks autonomy.

Though burdened with a list of ten impressive sounding functions, the NCW Bill 1990, grants the NCW few corresponding powers. It lacks the authority granted under the Commission of Enquiry Act to investigate lapses in legal violations. The NCW's five members (from different walks of life), under a chairperson sitting in Delhi, are unlikely to implement the ambitious "aims" even in the single area of equal payment of wages.

Further, the government's role remains ambiguous. The earlier power granted to the centre to terminate the services of the members before the expiry of the three-year term has been curtailed. But the government has reserved the right to "direct" the Commission's activities.

Rather than splitting hairs, these objections are particularly relevant within a national scenario where the government itself is one of the largest defaulters in implementing laws relating to women. Government violations of the Equal Remuneration Act (ERA) that applies to female agricultural workers or the failure to give justice to the victims of custodial rape are cases in point.

Apart from these objections to its form, what is needed is a realistic appraisal of the concept of a commission on women. Its highly centralised structure is likely to force the NCW to tread the path of umpteen other such bodies that have deliberated issues concerning women for many years, spending public money and wasting the time of well-qualified persons to produce volumes of information and recommendations, which are duly acknowledged by the government and then conveniently forgotten.

We have no dearth even now of such valuable information. What is lacking is implementation.

Backed by hare evidence, it is grass-roots level women's organisations who already monitor and analyse loopholes in law and policy. Only recently, in its attempt to get justice for two women who died of burns in suspicious circumstances, one such group was hampered in its collection of evidence by its inability to get a copy of the *post mortem* report. Under existing criminal law, the document can only be released to "next of kin". It is such organisations that need to be empowered rather than a top-heavy body with a centralised structure.

An honest and sincere effort to implement objectives that are already on paper is what is really needed. Apart from attempts to shift the existing bias in policy and law, this was the goal for which the National Commission for Women was first conceived. In its present form, the government's answer to 15 years of struggle by the women's movement is a worthless token. Aborted before being born.

(Editorial, *Business India*, September 17-30, 1990)

## YOUTH

### Promises and Precepts

* Many of the ills, that we are suffering from, have their genesis in the decline of national character, intellectual degeneration and the disappearance of a sense of discipline. To rejuvenate the society with influx of dedicated youth, special emphasis will be laid on moral and physical education of the young, along with their intellectual evolution. Time-tested programmes of N.C.C., N.S.S., participation in literacy campaign, Bharat Scouts and Guides, etc., shall be given added impetus.

Special efforts will be made to promote sports and games among the youth and enhance the prestige and honour of India in the national and international sports and games. Schemes will be developed to catch the young with potentials, talent and train them in sports and co-curricular activities.

To promote self-employment among the educated and skilled youth, a low interest loan of Rs 50,000 will be provided, along with a scheme for training in appropriate trades and crafts and necessary infrastructural support.

** Youth will be involved in national reconstruction and special schemes will be devised to ensure employment and their all-round development.

### Process of Action

A National Youth Council has been envisaged and the Prime Minister wrote a letter on October 6, 1990 to leaders of all political parties recognised by the Election Commission at the national level and the

State level, asking them to nominate their representative for the Council.

The letter points out that the question before us is how to motivate the youth in order to inculcate in them a pride and awareness of our heritage and to imbue them with a passion for social justice and patriotic fervour.

## ZIGZAGS

### Internal Squabbles of the Janata Party

#### *Resignations and Withdrawals*

On June 12, Three Ministers — Shri Arun Nehru, Shri Arif Mohammad Khan and Shri Satpal Malik — resigned from the National Front Government led by Prime Minister V. P. Singh. Their resignations were in protest against the reinduction of Shri Om Prakash Chautala as Haryana Chief Minister which in their opinion was contrary to all values they had propounded in their fight against the Congress.

On July 14, six ministers namely Shri Chimanbhai Mehta, Minister of State for Human Resource Development, Shri Subodh Kant Sahay, Minister of State for Home, Shri Bhajuman Behera, Minister of State for Petroleum, Shri Bhagey Goverdhan, Minister of State for Planning and Programme Implementation, Shri Anil Shastri, Deputy Finance Minister and Shri Ajay Singh, Deputy Minister for Railways resigned.

On July 15, 1990, Shri V.P. Singh, Prime Minister sent his resignation to the National Front Chairman, Shri N.T. Rama Rao and the Janata Dal President Shri R.S. Bommai. Following is the text of the letter:

> "The rationale of my being in the office of the Prime Minister was the trust of the people, of the members of National Front and the supporting parties.
>
> The developments during the last two days have shown that I have lost this trust.
>
> The rationale of my continuing in office is no longer there."
>
> Bowing to the general sentiments I wish to step down from the prime ministership.
>
> I have always held that for upholding a democratic norm an office

can be sacrificed.

I would request you to call a meeting of the National Front/Janata Dal Parliamentary Party to elect a new leader.

This should be done at the earliest so that uncertainty does not prevail at a time when the country is facing deep problems in Jammu and Kashmir, Punjab and on the border.

I would have sent my resignation to the President but in absence of an alternative leader of the National Front and the Janata Dal it would have paved the way for the comeback of the Congress(I) which also the people do not want. Hence the urgency of the election of a new leader."

A late-night meeting on July 15, 1990, attended by the Prime Minister and his Cabinet colleagues, members of the party's Political Affairs Committee and four Janata Dal Chief Ministers, endorsed the party President, Shri S. R. Bommai's categorial refusal to accept Shri Singh's resignation, which was given to him earlier in the day.

Shri V. P. Singh on Sunday, the 15th July, 1990, agreed to stay on as Prime Minister, in deference to the wishes of the National Front leaders but set a deadline for the Janata Dal President, Shri S. R. Bommai, to resolve Chautala Affairs by 16th July, 1990.

On July 15, 1990, Shri I. K. Gujral, the External Affairs Minister, Shri Harikishore Singh, Deputy External Affairs Minister, Shri Ram Pujan Patel, the Minister for Food and Civil Supplies and Shri Arangil Shreedharan, resigned from the Union Cabinet over the Chautala Affair. With this number of Union Minister who have resigned in protest against the reinduction of Shri Chautala as Harayna Chief Minister rose to 13.

On June 17, 1990, Prime Minister V. P. Singh rejected the resignation of all the 13 Ministers of his Cabinet. It may be recalled that these ministers had resigned on the induction of Shri Om Prakash Chautala as Chief Minister of Haryana.

*Criticism of the N.F. Government by Devi Lal, Former Deputy Prime Minister*

Text of Shri Devi Lal's letter to the Janata Dal President:

September 30, 1990

My Dear Shri Bommai,

I am writing this letter with deep distress and heart felt anguish over the way our young boys and girls, even in their early teens, are sacrificing their dear lives by self-immolation, consuming poison or otherwise. These young hopes of the future have taken to this extreme step by one hurried and unplanned decision of our Government of implementing the recommendations of the Mandal Commission report. I am led to believe that no proper discussion was held either in the Cabinet or the party or with the supporting parties of our minority Government, before the announcement. The undue haste and abandoning the process of consensus approach of deciding such a momentous issue is the very root cause of the whole problem today. This has even led the Press to impute motives to the sincerity of the Government in implementing the recommendations of the Mandal Commission report and even the so called friends of the Government in the Press reacted critically to the decision.

Let me make it clear at the very outset that I am not, repeat not, opposed to the upliftment of our unfortunate brothers and sisters belonging to the backward communities. I, in fact, started my political career with a protest against the treatment meted out to one of the members of the backward community.

I continued the struggle for their welfare throughout my life along with the leaders like Shri Karpoori Thakur of the depressed classes and backward communities. I as a member of the drafting committee of the Janata Dal election manifesto fully understood the implications of including the demand in the manifesto and had also stated in the Lok Sabha. I am not therefore opposed to the idea of the Mandal Commission recommendations but am opposed to the style, timing and the manner of announcing the acceptance of the recommendations and the mishandling of the whole issue.

The announcement of the acceptance of the recommendations on August 7, 1990 was an abortive attempt to scuttle the chances of the success of August 9, 1990 rally at Boat Club.

Some of the members of the Government seem to have thought, and accordingly misadvised the Prime Minister, that the announcement with one stroke will take away a major chunk of my sympathisers and friends away from me and the rally shall collapse, little knowing that the announcement will also immediately divide the whole society into two factions — the pro-Mandalities and the anti-Mandalities — thus preparing a ground for the civil war in every village, every town, every mohalla and every street. The fire was further fanned by two Cabinet Ministers by their open call to their sympathisers to come on the streets and fight their opponents. It is unheard of in the history of our country, nay of any country, the Cabinet Minister have instigated a section of the people to take to streets to silence those expressing their grievances. No Government can afford to divide its own people just to carry its views across. All my efforts to request the Prime Minister to dissuade one of his Cabinet colleagues from going to Jaipur and addressing the meeting there proved to be a naught. The visit further deteriorated conditions there and the Minister had to face the public wrath.

I expected the Prime Minister to rise above the petty personal prejudices and to give a healing touch by opening a dialogue with the agitating students and try to remove their misconceptions. However, his broadcast to the nation on September 26, 1990 fell far short of the expectations of the young students. He on the one hand stuck to his early stand of not diluting the recommendations and even talked of the resignation and on the other invited the students for discussion with an "open mind". This duplicity, coupled with insensitivity of the Government to the problem of the children have further estranged them, and in spite proper channel for the dialogue with the agitating students have been opened thus creating an impasse. The young lives are being lost, the property worth millions is being destroyed, the law and order situation has collapsed, the credibility of the Government to govern has been shattered and it has failed even to provide drinking water to 80 lakh population in the Capital. All this because a decision was taken at a wrong moment and without taking the consensus of all concerned.

I am a loyal and disciplined worker of the party and have contributed my little bit in the formation of the party and also of the Government. I have been keeping my silence all these days because of the party discipline and also that any move on my part may not be misunderstood and misinterpreted. But the time comes when the inner voice of your conscience compels you to rise above your party affiliations and your personal whims and prejudices. The time, I feel, is now. Though it is very sad for me to part company especially from the friends in the Government which has come into being by my efforts still I cannot support the Government which is so insensitive to the cries of the dying children and is leading the country to balkanisation and the society to pragmentation. I have, therefore, decided to relinquish my membership of the Lok Sabha. I am enclosing my resignation with the request that the same may be forwarded to the

Speaker of the Lok Sabha for acceptance with immediate effect.

(*Hindustan Times*, October 1, 1990)

*Janata Dal Dissident's Criticism*

Janata Dal dissident MPs' spokesman Yashwant Sinha said on October 6, 1990 that through their campaign the dissidents were able to draw the attention of the people and the party towards the Government failure on all fronts and to the fact that the "Prime Minister's chair is important enough for Shri V. P. Singh to stick to it at all costs."

Asked about the success of the dissidents' campaign against the Prime Minister, Shri Sinha said "we have succeeded in making the point we set out to make."

The dissident leader said none from the other camp had cared to reply to the points made by him at the National Front Parliamentary Party meeting on September 30, 1990 and in the joint letter sent by the dissidents to the Prime Minister seeking his resignation.

There were only remarks against the dissidents but no substantive rejoinder. "The debate is on issues but they want to reduce the debate to the numbers game," he said. Shri Sinha said he was prepared to listen to the replies on the issues raised by the dissidents.

Shri Sinha said the dissidents' campaign was on and he had no information whether the party leadership contemplated any disciplinary action against him.

Shri Sinha recently released the dissidents' letter signed by 29 party MPs. Five of them have since expressed faith in the Prime Minister and there are another five who are said to be holding the same view.

Asked about the chief failures of the Government as perceived by the dissidents, Shri Sinha said there was "total non-performance". He said every government had some good patches and bad patches but in the last 10 months, the story of this Government was that of one failure after the other and one crisis after the other.

He said when a government changed, there always arose hopes and aspirations of the people. For example, regarding Punjab, the Janata Dal was so vociferous about settling the issue but nothing was achieved. The situation had gone from bad to worse. A "historic" opportunity was lost, he said.

In Assam, the All Assam Students Union was on the warpath, besides the ULFA. There was failure in implementing the Assam accord. "We should have got something to show by way of implementation of the accord," he said.

On the Ram Janmabhoomi issue the party had said that it would respect the Hindu sentiment and that the temple might be built but there would be no harm to the mosque. The party was for a court settlement. Since the Bharatiya Janata Party support to the Government was not based on a minimum common programme, it was known that the temple issue could have become a critical one. The party should have done something about.

Today, Shri Sinha said, not even the basic issues had been framed in the court and no effort had been made to expedite the court verdict. The Government could have moved petitions. There had been only sterile discussions. Later the sub-committee on harmony met and its conclusions were leaked forcing the BJP to stay from the National Integration Council (NIC). Even the dialogue of religious leaders suggested by the Shankaracharya of Kanchi was being started after a lapse of 10 days. The point was whether even a day be lost on such an issue.

The Vishwa Hindu Parishad made its plans known to the Prime Minister and the Prime Minister asked for four months. Nothing happened even after eight months. Similarly, the situation in Jammu and Kashmir was bungled and the Governor was rewarded with a Rajya Sabha seat. There were one lakh Tamil refugees from Sri Lanka where a genocide was on, he said.

The functioning of the Government showed a casual approach and there was absolutely no evidence of the competence of the Government to solve the problem. Shri Sinha said the dissidents were not making any personal demand that it could be met by some gesture. The dissidents had waited enough before moving in the direction they did. The dissidents' demand was in the interest of the party only, he said.

(*Hindustan Times*, October 8, 1990)

*Shri Chandra Shekhar*

Shri Chandra Shekhar when asked whether he was also likely to meet the Prime Minister — on the same pattern Shri Devi Lal had his discussions with the Prime Minister — Shri Shekhar asked "meeting for what?" "If it was for discussing the national issues, what was there left to be discussed. They have already bungled in every sphere during the last 10 months," he said.

"It is not that I have not been giving my views to the Prime

Minister or meeting him," he said, but the Government performance had been dismal in every area: Punjab, Kashmir, Assam, Mandal Commission. "Their latest immoral act is in Karnataka," he said.

Shri Chandra Shekhar said he had no prejudice against or preference for anyone. Whatever he believed, he said expressed himself on several occasions, he said. "Let me make it clear: I don't want any personal adjustment with the Government," he said.

Having said so, he said, there was no scope for talks. "I have already given my views. If there is any change of attitude in the Prime Minister, so far I don't see anything. If there is any, then I will see," he said.

Shri Chandra Shekhar was in rage over the charge of the VP-loyalists that he was frustrated. "Where was the question of the frustration. I myself refused to join the Government," he said.

About the action in Karnataka, Shri Shekhar criticised the role of the Governor who entered "the fray" much earlier than he should have. Also, Shri Shekhar questioned the propriety of a senior party leader in offering party support to Shri Veerendra Patil.

(*Hindustan Times*, October 14, 1990)

*Janata Dal General Secretary*

The national general secretary of the Janata Dal and former Haryana Chief Minister Shri Om Prakash Chautala has squarely blamed the Prime Minister Shri V.P. Singh, for the prevailing chaotic conditions in the country.

Addressing a workers meeting in the local Yasin Park. Shri Chautala said that "Mr V.P. Singh is a hypcirite who talks of values when it came to judge others and threw to the winds, ethics and morality, when it came to save his 'gaddi'. Another prime minister in place of Shri Singh would have either resigned or would have been forced to quit by the Parliament, for the loss of hundreds of innocent lives and large-scale incidents of arson and violence by the pro-and anti-reservationists. His name would go down in the history as the man who provoked caste war in the country and sowed the seeds of disintegration in the Indian society."

Mr. Chautala felt that "had the Prime Minister consulted his Cabinet and the supporting parties, before announcing the implementation of the Mandal Commission report, things would not have gone out of hand, had the report not been implemented in an halfhearted manner. The reservation in jobs is a half-measure since it is not accompanied by reservations in professional institutions. Shri Chautala said and added that "in fact reservations is no way to improve the lot of the poor, because had it been so, the Harijans for whom reservations were made way back in 1952, would by now have become well-off."

To Shri Chautala, the only way to improve the lot of the poor is to improve their productivity, particularly of the farmers, as had been the thrust of the former Deputy Prime Minister, Shri Devi Lal's policies throughout. If the farmer is well off, the quality of life in other spheres will automatically improve.

(*Indian Express*, October 16, 1990)

**Handling of Major Issues by the NF Government**

Shri Nitish Chakravarty, in an article 'A Crisis of Confidence' *inter-alia* made these following observations:

The Government's clumsy handling of major issues facing the nation has strengthened doubts in the people's mind about its ability to pull itself out of the rut. In ten and a half months the National Front Government has stumbled from drift to indecision, from mistake to misadventure, triggering doubts about its competence to handle the country's multifarious problems. It has put its foot in its mouth over Sri Lanka. The Punjab imbroglio has got worse. A long winter or despair is ahead in terrorism-infested Kashmir. The prospect of being ruled by the United Liberation Front, Asom, in place of the elected Government looms large in the north-eastern State of Assam. The Rama temple controversy threatens to snowball into a fratricidal war. And the genie of the Mandal Commission report uncorked by the Prime Minister has the potential of plunging the nation into perennial caste conflicts.

Each one of these issues is so inflammable that once the people's wrath is aroused the Government would be hard put to survive. The euphoria over the Janata Dal's election victory last year is over, and its Government is in danger of crumbling under the pressure of *lok shakti* (peoples' might) which voted it to power less than a year ago. The image of a government is as good as the people perceive it to be; its credibility is measured not by its strength in Parliament but by the degree of confidence the people repose in its ability to deliver on its promises. The National Front Government is not rated high on either count.

The Government itself is to blame for throwing away the confidence people had reposed in it. Neither the man on the street nor the bureaucracy any longer sets much store by its words and actions. V.P. Singh's hasty decision to enforce the Mandal formula of 27 per cent reservations for OBCs is perceived essentially as a rearguard action to reinforce his defences against sniping by an estranged Devi Lal and hostile Chandra Shekhar. Few are taken in by the protestations of his commitment to uplifting those who are the social and educational underlogs.

Nitish Chakrvarty also added that "V.P. Singh's woes stem not so much from attacks by the Opposition as from the sustained smear campaign by a section of the leaders of the party he founded three years ago."

(*Frontline* October 13-26, 1990)

**Views of National Front Supporting Political Parties**

*B.J.P.*

On October 16, 1990 the Bharatiya Janata Party (BJP) warned in no uncertain terms, that it would withdraw its support to the V.P. Singh-led minority National Front Government if the construction of the Ram Temple at the disputed site in Ayodhya is not permitted or the party chief, Shri L.K. Advani's *Rathyatra* is "disrupted".

A resolution to this effect was adopted at the emergency meeting of the BJP national executive at the party headquarters, . . . decision to boycott the all-party meeting convened by the Prime Minister, Shri Vishwanath Pratap Singh on October 16.

The national executive has also authroised the leader of the party's parliamentary party, Shri Atal Behari Vajpayee, to write to the President about the decision to withdraw the support if such an eventuality arises. The executive has taken, what seems to be, a final decision on possible withdrawal of support if the Government does not heed the BJP advice on the Ayodhya issue.

The BJP chief said there was no question of "supporting the Congress-I if his party's withdrawal resulted in possibility of return of a Congress-I government." Let there be a mid-term poll' he said, "The ball is not in the Government's court."

He said the Congress-I factor had restrained his party for long from taking decision on withdrawal of support. "But", he said, "there are limits". Some members of the national executive, he said, were, in fact, in favour of taking a decision on withdrawing support immediately. "But we decided to warn them (the Front government)," he said, "We have figured out all possibilities that can happen."

> Referring to the resolution which said the "performance of the Government was a total disappointment", Shri Advani said even when the BJP had decided to support the National Front Government, it had reservations about its capacity to deliver the goods. The reservations started four weeks before the Lok Sabha elections, after the seat adjustments, when Shri V.P. Singh refused to go to a platform to campaign for his candidate because the BJP was there, "We had told the National Front Government about the area of differences."
>
> (*Indian Express*, October 17, 1990)

*Communist Party of India (Marxist)*

The Communist Party of India (Marxist) does not want the downfall of the National Front Government and return of the Congress-I to power because the latter can never be an alternative to the former. West Bengal Chief Minister Jyoti Basu has said in an interviews.

Shri Basu told *Ganashakti*, his party's Bengali newspaper, "The NF Government has chalked up both successes and failures. We can never support the price policy the NF Government is following. We have tried to persuade to change the price policy. We are continuing our efforts to change economic policies. But, considering all aspects, we will say we do not want the NF Government to go and the Cong-I to come back."

Asked if the CPI-M was considering to withdraw its support to the Government, Shri Basu said, "The question does not arise. Ever since the NF Government came to power, our party had been saying we would render support if it implemented its election manifesto. We had been urging to implement particularly these measures on which there was unanimity with the parties supporting the Government from outside.

"We have protested against the manner in which the NF Government raised the prices of petrol and petroleum products and railway freight rates, pushing up the prices of all other commodities, and have tried to make it realise that the people burdened as they were with price rises during the Congress regime, would find further price rises unbearable. The Government has not so far appreciated the impact of the price rises. We are, however, continuing our efforts and building up public opinion to persuade the Government to change its policies."

"This however, does not mean that either we are withdrawing our support to the government or we do not want this Government to continue and the Cong-I to return to power. We want the Government to continue, to implement its programme and correct its mistakes. It has inherited a bankrupt economy from the Rajiv Gandhi Government. The latter has left behind a huge budget deficit and innumerable closed factories, a very difficult economic situation. All this, we are trying to persuade the Centre that revenue receipts can be raised without resorting to price rises. We are hoping that the Central Government will change its policy in future," Shri Basu added.

(*Indian Express*, September 28, 1990)

*Present Political Scene*

Prophecies of Apocalypse now must, of course, be avoided. But never before since the dawn of independence 43 years ago has the national scene been so grim and grave and frightening as it is today. The gory consequences of V.P. Singh's cynical decision to "Mandalise India" — who could have thought even a month ago that young people outraged by the Raja Saheb's decision to reserve 27 per cent of jobs for so-called backward castes would start setting themselves aflame in areas where there is absolutely no tradition of self-immolation? — have, for the present, overshadowed almost everything else. But the crisis this country of 850 million people faces goes far beyond the Mandal Commission's dangerously divisive recommendations which the minority government has converted into some kind of an immutable gospel. . . .

Punjab is certainly in much worse shape today than it was when V.P. Singh had that famous and now all but forgotten jeep-ride in Amritsar. A well-meaning but bumbling former cabinet secretary, appointed Punjab's governor in something of a hurry, all but called off all action against terrorists and made statements which warned the cockles of the Khalisthanis' hearts. His abrupt removal was perhaps unavoidable. . . .

Even this was nothing compared with the unholy mess the Janata

Dal government has made on the issue of fresh elections in Punjab. The Cabinet first decided magisterially that the elections would be held in the luckless state at all costs. Then it did a sudden about-turn and took steps to amend the Constitution to extend President's rule in Punjab by another year. . . .

Leave alone the . . . thinking on Punjab, they behaved exactly the same way over the life-and-death situation in Kashmir during the first few months of this year. At that time, the then governor of the State, Jagmohan, the hurriedly named minister for Kashmir affairs, George Fernandes, and the home minister. Mufti Mohammad Sayeed, were not only talking but also working at cross-purposes. And yet, not once did the Prime Minister call in the threesome for a heart-to-heart talk and agreed decisions!

Even on the Mandal Commission's report the story is equally messy. A meeting of the full cabinet on the morning of August 7, 1990 authorised V.P. Singh to make his ill-conceived announcement on Mandal, principally to forestall the rally of dismissed Devi Lal. . . . After the public outcry against the manoeuvre, a meeting of the Cabinet's Political Affairs Committee was deeply divided over what has now become an almost literally burning issue.

Let us now turn to the second major malaise built into the present political dispensation from which there is going to be no early escape. It is that India's government is, in the words of a perceptive foreign diplomat, a "138/530" government.

The tragedy is that neither V.P. Singh, as Prime Minister, nor Rajiv Gandhi, as leader of the opposition as well as of the largest single party in the Lok Sabha who hopes to lead the government again some day, is mindful of the imperatives of the situation that obtains.

In the present circumstances, if national interest is not to be sacrificed to petty partisan considerations and implacable personal hatreds, both sides have to reach a modicum of consensus on some vital issues. . . . Unfortunately, this is not so. On the contrary, so great is the penchant for the game of political one-up-manship that national interest can go to hell. There can be no other explanation for the pettyfogging and pointless correspondence over Punjab between the Raja and Rajiv. . . .

Another manifestation of the same process at work is that Rajiv is lambasting V.P. Singh for unleashing caste warfare on the one hand and, on the other, taunting him for not extending the reservations for backward castes to the armed forces, institutions of science and technology and so on. . . .

The BJP is fed up with V.P. Singh. It is using the sentiment over the Rama temple at Ayodhya to mobilise countrywide support for itself. It has served notice that in the next election it would go it alone, leaving the Raja and the Janata Dal to stew in their own juice. But it does not want an early election. The position of the leftists is even more pathetic. They think the present dispensation is their best bet to keep themselves in power in their bastion, West Bengal. For the first time, they have got a say in the running of the Central Government. If the present government goes, they stand to lose more than they are doing as a result of having to acquiesce in the Janata Dal's waywardness.

The crowning irony of the situation is that an early fall of the present government does not suit even the Congress party, desperately anxious though it is to lay hands once again on the privileges and perquisites of power and pelf. . . .

In Madhu Limaye's apt words, the present government will limp along. This makes it all the more necessary to have to look at issues and problems which could cause a greater havoc than prevails already.

All this while we have been lamenting purely political woes. Not a word has been said about the foundation on which rests the entire political superstructure everywhere. India's economy is in one hell of a mess. It will worsen as a result of the Gulf crisis and the defence costs being imposed on us by Pakistan and by escalating needs of internal security, with the army being called out in town after town. But then that is a separate story.

(Inder Malhotra, *Competition Success Review*, November 1990)

**Politics of National Parties**

Had Mahatma Gandhi been alive he would probably have undertaken a death-fast to shame the nation's politicians back into their senses. For the political power struggle that has now begun to spread across the land, and the forces and symbols with which the antagonists are fuelling it, are making an insane mockery of the Mahatma's struggle to instill a sense of dignity and social purpose in his countrymen. Once again, even as the fortnight came to a close, the nation found itself up to its neck in the quicksand of caste and religion, and sinking slowly. . . .

But this country and its problems are more than just manipulable vote banks. The nation is more than just Uttar Pradesh and Bihar. And its people when roused by a wave can upset the best of calculations.

But what a price it is having to pay. Right now the wave sweeping this land is that of negative politics in which the leaders at the helm of affairs seem to have lost sight of the national perspective and emerged as petty manipulators more interested in one-up-manship than the larger common good.

The real issues facing the nation, its fundamental agonies, are conveniently forgotten. The law and order situation deteriorates steadily all over with the inexorable march of the gun. Rising prices are crippling the livelihoods of the majority of Indians. Health and family planning programmes are in disarray. The industrial policy languishes in uncertainty. Corruption at the grassroots level — rural banks, ration shops, housing societies, government recruitment — plays havoc with the basic needs of the common man, Punjab burns. Kashmir burns.

Even as the nation is torn asunder by these problems, the country's politicians, instead of addressing these issues, or taking clear stands on them and guiding the nation through its period of darkness are busy in blindfolding it. Their interest is besting their rivals and clamouring aboard crudely-crafted vote-wagons. In this atmosphere the major national parties are losing their relevance.

This was in ample evidence at the recently-concluded meeting of the National Integration Council, the one body where national leaders convene to consider common goals in the interest of the integrity of the country. Every so-called leader — Rajiv Gandhi, Chandra Shekhar, Jyoti Basu, N.T. Rama Rao — used this forum not to deal collectively and rationally with the real pains of the country but to score embarrassing points against one another, and settle scores through small-minded gestures and public relations gimmicks.

A period of darkness and destructive confrontation has besieged the land in which its leaders, instead of finding solutions, have become the creators of problems.

(Inderjit Badhwar and Prabhu Chawla, *India Today*, October 15, 1990)

**An Applause: New Rail Act**

The new Railways Act, 1989, which repeals the old Act of 1890, has not come a day too soon. Why the old Act was allowed to drag on for so long with only amendments added to it over a period of time can be explained only by the Railway Ministry, which handles one of the largest rail traffics in the world. The most noteworthy feature of the new Act is the doubling of the amount of compensation for deaths in rail accidents. Instead of Rs. 1 lakh, it has been raised to Rs. 2 lakh; rail employees on duty killed in accidents will also be entitled to get the same amount. The liability for scheduled injuries in accidents has also been doubled and will now range between Rs. 16,000 and Rs. 2 lakh. The word "dependent" has been redefined to include the parents of even a minor killed in an accident. Stringent punishments provided in the Act for misusing railway facilities such as alarm chain pulling, carrying dangerous substances in the train compartments or travelling without tickets or unauthorisedly transferring reserved tickets are meant to deter potential offenders.

These changes in the law are certainly welcome provided they are strictly enforced. Earlier experience in this regard has been rather disappointing. Drinking alcoholic beverages is "strictly" prohibited in trains but the directive is invariably defied with impunity specially in prestigious trains like Rajdhani Express and De Luxe trains by regular passengers in connivance with the catering staff. Alarm chain pulling with the intention of misuse now carries a fine of Rs. 1000 or imprisonment or both, while the penalty for transferring a ticket is Rs. 500 or imprisonment of up to three months. The latter is apparently to curb the unauthorised sale of tickets by touts to needy passengers for a premium. Even negligently crossing of unmanned level crossings is deemed to be an offence under the new Act. This provision will have to be publicised in the rural areas and in small towns where people still use railway level crossings as a legitimate thoroughfare.

(*Hindustan Times*, June 30, 1990)

**National Government**

On October 19, 1990 Sheikh Abdul Rehman, secretary-general of the state unit of Janata Dal, called for setting up a national government at the Centre to deal with the numerous problems facing the country.

Addressing newspersons here, Sheikh Abdul Rehman said that the current economic crisis, the rising prices and the recent growth of fundamentalism, along with the problems which were already there, had created "a very difficult situation".

As these problems required collective effort by all political parties, the Prime Minister, Shri V.P. Singh, should revive his idea of forming a National Government, Sheikh Rehman said.

(*Indian Express*, October 21, 1990)

## ZIP: PATHWAYS AND CORRECTIVE MEASURES

### Fundamental Duties*

51A. *Fundamental duties* — It shall be the duty of every citizen of India –

(a) to abide by the Constitution and respect its ideals and institutions, the National Flag and the National Anthem;
(b) to cherish and follow the noble ideals which inspired our national struggle for freedom;
(c) to uphold and protect the sovereignty, unity and integrity of India;
(d) to defend the country and render national service when called upon to do so;
(e) to promote harmony and the spirit of common brotherhood amongst all the people of India transcending religious, linguistic and regional or sectional diversities; to renounce practices derogatory to the dignity of women;
(f) to value and preserve the rich heritage of our composite culture;
(g) to protect and improve the natural environment including forest, lakes, rivers and wild life, and to have compassion for living creatures;
(h) to develop the scientific temper, humanism and the spirit of inquiry and reform;
(i) to safeguard public property and to abjure violence;
(j) to strive towards excellence in all spheres of individual and collective activity so that the nation constantly rises to higher levels of endeavour and achievement.

### Pathways and Corrective Measures

*Gandhiji on Characteristics of Clean Life*

1. Truth

*Ins. by the Constitution (Forty-second Amendment) Act, 1976, s. 11. (w.e.f. 3-1-1977).

2. Non-Violence
3. Celebacy
4. Control of the palate
5. Non-stealing
6. Non-possession
7. Swadeshi
8. Fearlessness
9. Non-touchability.

*Aspects of Clean Life*

1. *Man and his self*. This implies–

   (a) Self-control and self-discipline.
   (b) Living within one's means.
   (c) Simple living and high thinking.
   (d) Earning by honest means.

2. *Man and his work*. This means–

   (i) Working honestly.
   (ii) Working with whole-hearted devotion.
   (iii) Working in a spirit of non-detachment.

3. *Man and his fellow-men*. This includes–

   (a) Relation based on love, mutual understanding and appreciation.
   (b) Goodwill towards all.

4. *Man and his environment*. This incorporates–

   Care and nature of nature and ecology from which man derives great benefit.

5. *Man and his technology*. This includes–

   (i) Use of technology for human welfare.
   (ii) Technology as a servant and not a master.
   (iii) Harmonising technological and ethical values.

*Nehru on Fundamentals of Social Behaviour*

1. In spite of political differences, everyone should unite for the defence and well-being of the country and co-operate with others to implement programmes for the common good.
2. The unity and good of the nation should be given first importance and people should, therefore, rise above differences of caste, creed, language and province, and think more of the country as a whole.
3. Violence of any kind must be shunned and avoided. Violence creates hatred and is disruptive.
4. Religion is meant to raise an individual and to make him tolerant of others. Narrow prejudices and intolerance do not create respect for one's own religion in the eyes of others. We should honour not only our own religion but the religions of others also.
5. We should aim at equality of treatment and avoid feelings of high and low.
6. We should aim at becoming good citizens, subordinating self-interest and aiming at the common good.
7. Women should be treated with respect and as comrades. They should not be kept in *purdah* or seclusion, but given opportunities to participate in national activities.
8. Children should be treated with affection and gentleness and not beaten or scolded.
9. Liquor and all other intoxicants should be avoided.
10. Village and cottage industries should be encouraged, and as far as possible khadi should be used.
11. Adulteration of foodstuffs and other articles must be prevented.
12. The giving or accepting of bribes is bad, both for the giver and taker, and must be vigorously dealt with.
13. The house, street and village or town should be kept neat and clean.
14. We should try to understand the great developmental work that is going on in the country, such as the Five Year Plan, the community development schemes, etc., and co-operate in functioning and implementing it.
15. Manual labour should be respected and everyone should endeavour to engage himself in some form of manual labour for constructive work.

Pt. Jawahar Lal Nehru
(*An Appeal to the People of India*, 1959)

## Duties, Concepts and Characteristics of Rulers

### *Duties of Rulers*

1. Ruler is the remover of the difficulties of the people. *(Yajurveda* 7-35)
2. Ruler should hear the grievances of the people. *(Yajurveda* 33-15)
3. Oh Ruler, never tell a lie, shun abusive language and be not angry! (*Yajurveda* 8-23)
4. Ruler should have control over his tongue. (*Yajurveda* 23-43)
5. Ruler should encourage art, industry and trade in his realm. He should arrange for irrigation projects and encourage production. (*Yajurveda* 23-28)
6. Ruler should keep his foreign policy secret. (*Yajurveda* 9-24-27)
7. Ruler should measure the strength of his army. (*Yajurveda* 11-22)
8. Ruler should send his envoys to the other countries. (*Atharvaveda* A 8-87, *Rigveda* 7-67-7)
9. Ruler should make arrangements for training the army. (*Yajurveda* 17-33)
10. Ruler should look after the welfare of his soldiers. (*Atharvaveda* A 10-5-44-65).
11. Ruler should make arrangements for manufacture of weapons. (*Yajurveda* 16-26)
12. Ruler should make transport arrangements. (*Yajurveda* 29-48)
13. Ruler should defeat his enemy. (*Yajurveda* 27-37).
14. Ruler, should spread brave and loyal soldiers in all directions! (*Yajurveda* 16-6).
15. Ruler, should protect the women and children of those soldiers who have died fighting in war. (*Yajurveda* 18-77).
16. Ruler should punish the guilty, the wicked, the degraded and the immoral. (*Yajurveda* 23-21)
17. Ruler who squeezes money from his subjects wrongly should be removed. (*Yajurveda* 22-31).
18. Ruler should take the advice of his ministers in all state affairs. (*Yajurveda* 17-24).

*Concept of an Efficient Administrator*

He is full of youthful energy and accomplishes his objective with a sharp intellect and quick decisions. His behaviour is couched in truthful dealings. he is prominent among the virtuous ones. He is easily approachable but is like a swift-moving cloud. He is protector of all. he readily pays back all his obligations. His touches are like the cool breeze and he showers bliss on all.

(*Rigveda*, 1-87).

*Characteristics of the Rulers*

1. Liberality, generosity, charity.
2. A high moral character.
3. Sacrificing everything for the good of the people.
4. Honesty and integrity.
5. Kindness and gentleness.
6. Austerity in habits.
7. Freedom from hatred, ill-will and enmity.
8. Non-Violence.
9. Patience, forbearance, tolerance and understanding.
10. Non-obstruction, non-opposition. The rulers should not obstract any measures that are conducive to the welfare of the people.

(*Jataka*)

**Characteristics and Value Orientation of a Public Servant**

*Characteristics*

1. follows rules and regulations strictly.
2. does not show any favour to anyone for any consideration.
3. comes to office in time and works there till the prescribed hours of duty.
4. spends every second of his office time on the assigned work.
5. does not do any personal work and does not meet any social or personal obligation during office hours.
6. does not use any item of office stationary (not even pins) for personal work.
7. does not avail of the services of any member of the staff for personal work.

8. does not use official telephone (in the office or residence) for personal or social calls.
9. does not accept gifts in cash or kind on any occasion from the beneficiaries.
10. does not do any private business with those having official dealings.

*Value Orientation*

According to P.K. Doraiswamy (*The Hindu*, August 18, 1987), subject to marginal adjustments, the public administrators fall into various categories as shown below with regard to their basic value-orientation (ignoring for the present, competence etc.):

| *Category* | *In Percentage* |
|---|---|
| (a) Colluders and self-seekers | 15 |
| (b) Indifferent, low motivation | 15 |
| (c) Those who possess an average sense of duty, morality, etc., and want to a peaceful, uneventful career; willing to acquiesce in if pressurised | 50 |
| (d) High motivation and commitment falling short of facing martyrdom | 15 |
| (e) Idealists willing to face martyrdom | 5 |
| Total | 100 |

**Administrative Inefficiency and Wastage in Government**

Faulty organisation, wastage in public expenditure and corruption, lack of rapport and inefficiency coupled with slackness are some of the glaring flaws of our present day administration.

The administration is top-heavy and most of the departments have "the millstone of excessive staff" round their necks.

The departments fetching revenues are being run on unsound commercial lines with the result that the receipts are shrinking and the expenditure growing. The fat salaries and enormous perks drawn by the higher officers and especially those of the Public Enterprises are a great drain. Practically, there is little check on them. They behave like Great Mughals, thought most of the Public Enterprises have practically no competition, they incur heavy losses.

*Inefficiency in Administration*

The bureaucracy has turned indifferent to the ideas of administrative reforms which, if implemented, will necessarily involve the dilution of its vast powers. It is also creating fresh problems — and solving of them later — to enhance its reputation.

The Government has acquired a strange style of functioning — first to prolong consideration of genuine demands, then drive the employees to resort to strike, and finally redress their grievances.

It is an admitted fact that the bureaucracy has generally acted as a stumbling block and has seldom accepted the genuineness of grievances in the normal course.

We are multiplying departments at various levels with each doing little more than creating work for the other.

The administrative set-up of the country is top-heavy.

The Civil Servants, by and large, have been left unbridled.

Two bureaucrats in place of one don't make administration twice as efficient.

The bureaucrats manage to have enormous privileges.

The enormous number of writ petitions, that are pending in Administrative Tribunals, High Courts and the Supreme Court, and which have arisen out of dissatisfaction of civil servants against the orders of Executive Government (Senior Civil Servants), is perhaps due to *ad hoc* administration decisions taken by the Senior Civil Servants. None seems to be accountable for this state of affairs.

*Rs. 10 Per Sheet of Paper Typed*

. . .Officials in New Delhi point out that a typist, who types six pages in a day (apparently the average in some offices), costs the Government Rs. 10 per sheet of paper typed.

(*India Today*, March 15, 1987)

*1000 Houses, Shops Bulldozed in Delhi*

This was the headlines of a news item in *The Hindustan Times*, dated June 21, 1987. This raises many important issues? Why did the concern authorities allow such construction? Were they unconcerned or were hand in glove with the defaulters? The obvious answer is they had some interest. The concerned officers gained on both the occasions, i.e., at the time of unauthorised construction and at the time of demolition.

*Government Waste*

Every third rupee spent in the country is spent by some government department or the other. That is Rs. 100,000 crore a year. And every fifth rupee out of that goes waste; Rs. 20,000 crore a year, Rs. 4 lakh down the drain every minute.

Following are the laws of Government waste:

1. Some departments are born wasteful, some achieve wastefulness, and some have waste thrust upon them.
2. Forget the goal, it's the paper work that counts.
3. A programme expands to make complete use of the money available. (Money has got to be spent, therefore, it must be spent).
4. When in doubt set up a Committee.
5. Every bureaucrat rises beyond his level of incompetence.
6. When things go wrong, stonewall.
7. If a thing is worth doing, it is worth doing wastefully.
8. Time is money and more time is more money.
9. When trimming expenses, go for the pennies, not the pounds.
10. Ask not what you can do for Government; ask what the Government can do for you.
11. If Government money can be misappropriated, it will.
12. To make crime unprofitable, let the public sector run it.

(*India Today*, March 1987)

**How Corruption Spreads**

There are countless mini-Bofors in our daily life and we hardly take note of them. Total sums involved in the 'so-called' minor deviations and privileges run into thousands of crores of rupees. The existence of black money estimated at about Rupees forty crores in the country points out the existence of corruption on a large scale.

The following instances though look very minor, but have great significance in the broader context of corruption. It is seldom realised that a single deviation on the part of a V.I.P. and others in power leads to scores of deviations.

1. Use of staff car by a V.I.P. for transporting the tutor for his grand children. The car covered about 30 km daily. The driver of the car told this to half a dozen or so drivers working with the V.I.P. The tutor also told this to about 100 teachers working in the school. They further narrated this to their friends. In the process about one thousand people came to know it. Apart from petrol expenses to the extent of about Rs. 1000 p.m., over time allowance was paid to the driver. This raises the issue. If a V.I.P. can misuse his position, why not others?
2. Use of staff car by a V.I.P. for sending lunch to his son working in an office located at a distance of about 20 km from the office of the V.I.P. The car covered a distance of about 40 km daily. This involved an expenditure of about Rs. 1,000 p.m.
3. Use of staff car by a bureaucrat and a technocrat for coming and going to office — sometime 80 km daily — an expenditure of about Rs. 2,000 p.m. Over time of the driver to the extent of about Rs. 700 p.m. is also involved.
4. Deployment of dozens of vehicles and officers on the occasion of the marriage of a sons of a bureaucrat.
5. Use of 6 to 8 orderlies daily for personal work by a Commandant.
6. Nomination of the son of a V.I.P. to a professional college.
7. Use of unfair means in the examination by the ward of a V.I.P. with the collaboration of officers.
8. Finding out the fictitious Roll No. of the ward by a V.I.P. working in the same Board conducting the examination and approaching the concerned examiner for favours.
9. Removal of furniture and other items by a V.I.P. from his official residence to his personal residence.
10. Claiming T.A. and D.A. without inspecting schools.
11. Claiming remuneration from Board without visiting centres of examinations.
12. Using official machinery, i.e., Office Staff especially personal assistant, telephone, stationary etc. for personal benefit.
13. Acceptance of gifts in cash or kind for showing favour.
14. Out of turn allotment of cars, flats and hand etc. to V.I.P.'s etc.

There are thousands of such instances with which we come across daily and are involved directly or indirectly. But the pity is that very little notice is taken of these deviations. The fact however remains that these are the starting points of corruption.

**Likely Sources of Corruption and Favouritism**

1. Disregard for Moral Values.
2. Mad Race for money and material things.
3. Wealth as the Status Symbol.
4. Discretionary powers of V.I.P.'s, Ministers including Prime Minister and Chief Ministers, Senior Civil Servants and Technocrats etc.
5. Extensions and reappointments etc.
6. Appointment of retired Senior Civil Servants, Technocrats, Judges etc., as Ambassadors, High Commissioners, Governors etc.
7. Appointment of retired Senior Civil Servants and Judges on various Administrative and other Tribunals etc.
8. Centralised purchases in various Ministries and Departments.
9. Predominance of subjective elements in appointments, promotions, postings and transfers.
10. Adhocism in appointments and promotions etc.
11. Lack of accountability and especially at higher level posts.
12. Subjectivity in assessing income-tax, sales-tax, customs duties etc.
13. Flexibility in the issuance of licences, permits and quotas.
14. Too many laws and their faulty implementation.
15. Creation of Senior posts for accommodating favourites.
16. So-called privileges of the Higher Ups.
17. Delays in administering justice.
18. Ineffective Intelligence System.
19. Wide Disparity in the Powers of the Senior Civil Servants and Technocrats.
20. Too much concentration of power in the hands of the Senior Civil Servants.
21. Plethora of High-Sounding Institutions in different fields.
22. Lack of a proper sense of determining priorities.
23. Establishing institutions on the pattern of advanced countries but without following their work ethics.
24. Lack of effective check on the working of various Ministries, Departments etc.
25. Political System dependent upon huge money for elections.

26. Vast opportunities for Legislators for private gains.
27. Contribution to political parties and consequential favours.
28. False promises at the time of elections.
29. Non-stability of Ministries and Ministers.
30. Exploitation of caste, regional, and religious sentiments etc.
31. Inaugurations, stone-laying ceremonies etc. and resultant expenditure.
32. Frequent Public Rallies.
33. Too much dependence of Ministers on Civil Servants.
34. Lack of proper sense of public morality and accountability.

**Corrective Measures: Clean Life, Clean Politics and Clean Administration**

"Each work has to pass through three stages: ridicule, opposition and acceptance. Any one who things ahead of his time is bound to be misunderstood. So opposition and persecution are welcome. One has to be steady and pure and these will vanish."

— *Swami Vivekananda*

Each one of us, at one time or the other, feels distressed at the erosion of moral and ethical values in our country. Today if we want to impress the virtues like selflessness, sacrifice, honesty, truthfulness, patriotism, or the like; have we only to delve into history. Living examples in a particular field, say politics, administration or social work would be very difficult to quote.

Selfless workers still exist. Maybe, they are the hard core that has been sustaining our system. Their impact, however, is negligible.

According to the highest standard of ethical morality even the use of an 'office pin' for personal, political and social use is a corrupt practice. But then who cares for such ideals?

There is a legend about a Principal of a college who was so particular about public morality that he never used his 'office pen' in writing a personal letter.

The situation was different in the pre-independence era. There was galaxy of men like Gandhi, Nehru and Patel at the top who had the courage of their convictions. They lived and died for the causes dear to them. The few corrupt and dishonest were heavily out-numbered by them. Subhas Bose, Aurobindo or H.V. Kamath did not hesitate to resign from I.C.S. once they felt they had more meaningful things to do. People had the courage to renounce honours and titles, power and pelf to get into the struggle for independence that at that time had nothing to offer beyond jail terms, lathi charge, hardships and privations.

Gandhiji, throughout his life, strove to create a social order in which honour and prestige would be determined by what one sacrificed rather than acquired by way of material possessions. Bouquets were for those who burnt their foreign clothes and chose the coarse Khadi. Public honours were for those who abandoned the imported cars and marched on foot with the peasants and workers. Unfortunately the value system that Gandhiji and his devoted followers had so laboriously built started crumbling after Independence. Austerity, which at one time, was the hallmark of leadership became irrelevant. Gradually two sets of values got entrenched one for professing and the other for practising.

The malady did not remain confine to the politicians alone. Soon it spread among the bureaucrats and the professionals including businessmen, whoever got a chance. Today we are face to face with a situation in which each one is inclined to think of 'Self before Community', 'Rights without Responsibility', 'Recommendation rather than Rule of Merit.' Honest work is secondary. Privileges matter. Honest people are sometimes termed 'worldly unwise', 'cowards' and 'becharas' etc.

Honesty, if it is good as a principle, has also to be practised without exception. Whatever name or justification we give to deviations from honesty, it invariably means corruption irrespective of whether the deviations are by the State, someone highly placed, or one in general run.

Honesty, like virginity cannot be partial. As long as we have two standards of honesty — one to be practised by the common man and the other by highly placed persons — the former without exception and the latter with exceptions, we shall only have dishonesty in our political as well as social fabric. The lowest placed would obviously always rationalise his misdoing by pointing to the Head who is violating the rule under his exceptional powers. The office clerk carrying government stationery home would always explain his conduct by pointing to the boss who use his personal assistants, peons, staff car, telephone, etc., for personal errands. In this game of corruption and dishonesty more than four-fifths of the country's population is a loser. The fight against dishonesty has to be initiated from the TOP.

It is observed that generally Law Makers and Implementers become the Law Breakers.

It is very depressing to observe that the land of sages and seers — with a great spiritual past — is tending to become a land of mere pious sermonisers, tall talkers and hypocrites. Honest practitioners are very rare. What a great fall?

We are far away from accepting democracy as a way of life. It is seen working only for a few days at the time of elections when the voter is considered a 'sovereign'. Thereafter the 'sovereign' is reduced to almost a non-entity till next elections.

Political leaders including Ministers and Chief Ministers usually remain busy in the 'power game' and have very little time to attend to the problems of the common man.

Very often, the senior bureaucrats spend a good deal of their time in meeting social obligations, discussing promotional prospects, attending to the V.I.P.'s during office hours and looking for privileges. In such a situation the common man is left at the mercy of the lower rungs who have their own ways of doing things.

Religious and spiritual leaders confine themselves to learned discourses and hardly bother to stress various virtues of leading a clean life. Religion has, by and large, divorced itself from ethics and reality.

Over the years, the executive, has become more arbitrary; the judicial standards have suffered a decline; and Parliament, which has a major responsibility to run the affairs of the Nation, no longer enjoys the respect of the people, it should.

Why such a scenario! The answer is straight! Our top guides — leaders and senior bureaucrats and technocrats — have, by and large, failed to set higher standards of life in their day-to-day conduct. At least such an impression has been created in the minds of the masses.

It must be remembered that the holders of public office in a democracy should not only be above board but also appear to be so. One deviation on the part of a V.I.P. leads to thousands of deviations by followers.

A beginning could be made by adopting and giving a fair trial to the following measures:

Holders of High Office must exercise self-restraint and set highest standards of clean life. Much more good can come to the community if they perform their assigned functions efficiently and honestly rather than spend time on ceremonial inaugurations and speech making. They should adhere to strict 'No Exception Rule'. That would be the key to the success of any plan for eradication of corruption.

Maximum damage to public morality is done in the grey areas between Party and the Government. This demarcation should be distinct and violations must be made culpable irrespective of who does it. Corruption can be eradicated only if the corrupt do not get protection at the hands of the people in high authority.

Regular elections of the office-bearers of the political parties should be held.

The principle of public scrutiny of funds collected and spent by the government agencies needs to be extended to political parties and social organisations alike. Organisations and institutions spending beyond their known sources of income should be suspect as are individuals.

Government patronage to public institutions must be governed by objective criteria with no discretionary powers to dole out public funds. Similarly, use of public premises, conveyance, etc., must be on payment basis with no subsidy or differential rates.

Public dealings in all Government offices must be made time bound. The first competent authority must give its decision within one month failing which the advantage should go to the petitioner. Where necessary, additional staff may be employed subject to 'No Exception' rule.

The 'No Exception' rule when extended to areas of finance would reduce and retard the generation of black money. There should be no directives for purchase on price preference.

The existing practice of 'extensions' beyond the age of retirement in public interest should be done away with. The retiring head no longer cares to train a successor. Instead he takes pliant postures and advises soft options. The government get biased advice and the whole chain of persons due for promotion get demoralised. Talent is substituted by 'Yes-men'.

Ambassadors, Public Sector Heads, Governors, Chairmen and Members of various Commissions must come from serving professionals within the age of retirement. There is plenty that needs to be done in the area of Social Work and those interested in serving the public should do so without government status and perks.

The next on the list would be abolition of hidden perks and privileges available to persons in top brackets. Every one, including all V.I.Ps, must pay taxes as any body else under a common law without exceptions. Where necessary, the salaries may be raised but the public must know what the services of a person really cost the community.

Procedures for selection, promotion, appointment, transfer, etc., of public servants must be objective and open to scrutiny. Here again there should be no provision for exceptions as otherwise the emphasis would shift from efficiency to psycophancy. In no case, personal interviews should have more than 15 per cent weightage.

Investigations/Decisions in cases relating to V.I.Ps and Members of the Cabinet should be decided by Commissions/Benches of Courts consisting of not less than three judges.

Initiative must come from V.I.Ps, Leaders especially Political, Senior Bureaucrats, Technocrafts, Intellectuals, journalists, Professionals and Business Magnates.

### *A Final Word*

It is our NATION, the India of All of Us, that is at risk. It is the call of the hour to take up the challenge and resolve to see it through that India in the world will be secured. We, Indians, have succeeded in the past and so shall again.

## AFTERMATH

### **Overview**

#### *Chronology of Related Events*

August 1: Devi Lal sacked from Union Cabinet.
August 7: Government accepts Mandal Commission report.
September 25: L.K. Advani begins Rath Yatra.
October 19: Ordinance proclaimed to acquire disputed land.
October 21: The Ordinance is withdrawn.
October 22: CMs meet. Subcommittee formed to tackle Ayodhya issue.
October 23: Advani is arrested. BJP withdraws support. VP refuses to quit, says he'll prove majority in Parliament. Left promises to stand by VP. BJP, allied Hindu organisations give call for Bharat bandh.

#### *What They Say*

Shri R. Venkataraman, President: "The ball is in my court now".

Shri V.P. Singh, Prime Minister: "I will prove my majority on the floor of the House".

Shri A.B. Vajpayee: "V.P. Singh has declared war not only on BJP but on the Bharatiya Janata itself, that is the Indian people."

Shri L.K. Advani: (just before his arrest): "The tremendous goodwill generated by this yatra is a shining example of our tradition of national integration."

Shri V.N. Gadgil, Congress (I) : "This Government has been in the intensive care unit and now has gone into the termination ward".

Shiv Sena Chief, Bal Thackeray (in Bombay): "BJP's line is our line. As long as there are people like Shri V.P. Singh and Shri Mulayam Singh Yadav in power this (securing Hindu Rashtra) would be difficult to achieve".

Shri Salahuddin Owaisi (in Hyderabad): "The NF Government will survive . . . watch for the next few days."

Shri Chandra Shekhar, Janata Dal: "The arrest of a person of Shri Advani's stature is not something small."

Shri S.R. Bommai, Janata Dal President: "When we face Parliament (for proving majority) I am sure every party, every member will act according to conscience".

Uttar Pradesh CM Shri Mulayam Singh Yadav (in Etawah, U.P.): The Lok Sabha and Vidhan Sabha elections could be held simultaneously in the State if there was mid-term poll in the near future".

(*Hindu*, October 24, 1990)

*Party Position in Lok Sabha*

The latest party position in the Lok Sabha as on October 20, 1990 is as follows:

| Name of the Party/Group | Strength | Name of the leader |
|---|---|---|
| Congress(I) | 195 | Rajiv Gandhi |
| Janata Dal | 140 | V.P. Singh |
| BJP | 86 | L.K. Advani |
| CPI(M) | 33 | Somnath Chatterjee |
| CPI | 12 | Indrajit Gupta |
| AIADMK | 11 | R.Muthiah |
| SAD(M) | 5 | S.S. Mann |
| RSP | 4 | Nani Bhattacharya |
| AIFB | 3 | Chitta Basu |
| J&K National Conference | 3 | Saif-ud-Din Soz |
| BSP | 3 | Kumari Mayavati |
| JMM | 3 | |
| Shiv Sena | 3 | |

| Name of the Party/Group | Strength | Name of the leader |
|---|---|---|
| Telugu Desam | 2 | Vinaya Kumar Raju |
| Muslim League | 2 | Ibrahim Sulaiman Sait |
| IPF | 1 | |
| MGP | 1 | |
| Marx-Coord | 1 | |
| Congress(S) | 1 | |
| AIMEIN | 1 | |
| Kerala Congress(M) | 1 | |
| SSP | 1 | |
| ABHMS | 1 | |
| GNLF | 1 | |
| Independent | 10 | |
| Vacancies | 20 | |
| Total | 544 | (Excluding the Speaker) |

(*Statesman*, October 24, 1990)

### Withdrawal Ordinance

The President on October 23, 1990 issued the Ram Janmabhoomi-Babri Masjid (Acquisition of Area) Withdrawal Ordinance negating the earlier Ordinance and it "shall be deemed to have come into force on October 19, 1990.

The right, title and interest in relation to the Ram Janmabhoomi-Babri Masjid area, as specified in the earlier ordinance, "shall be deemed never to have been transferred to and vested in the Central Government".

Any suit, appeal or other proceeding, of whatever nature, in relation to any property in the temple-mosque area, pending before any court, tribunal or other authority, "shall be deemed never to have abated and such suit, appeal or other proceeding (including the orders or interim orders of any court thereon) shall be deemed to have been restored to the position existing immediately before the commencement of that Ordinance".

The appointment of any receiver in respect of the "whole or any part of the aforesaid property shall be deemed never to have been withdrawn.

"Any other action taken or thing done under the Ordinance shall be deemed never to have been taken or done.

"Subject to the provisions of Section 2, the Ram Janmabhoomi-Babri Masjid (Acquisition of Area) Ordinance, 1990, is hereby withdrawn, the new Ordinance said.

After a Cabinet meeting in the forenoon, the Prime Minister called on the President and apprised him of the circumstances in which the earlier Ordinance had to be withdrawn.

(*Statesman*, October 24, 1990)

**Arrest of BJP President, L.K. Advani**

The Bihar Government on October 23, 1990 arrested the BJP leader, Shri L.K. Advani, along with several party MPs and legislators. Shri Advani was arrested by the Border Security Force and the Central Reserve Police Force personnel at the Samastipur circuit house where he had arrived in his rath after addressing a number of meetings in north Bihar towns. He was flown in a helicopter to the Dummka district town of tribal Santhal Parganas from where he was taken to the Masenjore State Government rest house in an idyllic spot on the banks of the Ajay river on the West Bengal-Bihar border.

The Bihar Chief Minister, Shri Laloo Prasad Yadav, later told presspersons that Mr.Advani was arrested along with other BJP MPs, legislators and VHP workers under the National Security Act. . . .

According to highly placed sources, the arrests were made at the behest of the Prime Minister, Shri V.P. Singh. The Chief Minister, however, said the arrests had been ordered by him without consulting the Prime Minister as the maintenance of law and order was the responsibility of the State Government. Asked how long the arrested BJP leaders would be kept under detention, the Chief Minister replied cryptically that they would remain in jail as long as they did not "shed their religious fanaticism".

The Chief Minister accused the BJP and the VHP of hatching a "conspiracy" by whipping up religious frenzy under the cover of the Ram Rath Yatra. He said the Rath had been parked at Samastipur, the home district of the late Karpoori Thakur. He said he had treated Shri Advani and his convoy with the utmost respect and provided tight security to them.

(*The Hindu*, October 24, 1990)

**Reaction to Advani's Arrest**

Various political, religious and non-governmental organisations have sharply reacted to arrest of the BJP president. Shri L.K. Advani. While some have criticised the move as an act of treachery, others have welcomed it as a just move to defuse the tension created by the Ram Janmabhoomi-Babri Masjid issue.

*H.P. Chief Minister Shri Shanta Kumar*

The Himachal Pradesh Chief Minister Shri Shanta Kumar, strongly condemned the arrest of Shri Advani at a time when the Supreme Court had rejected the petition filed for stopping the Ram Rath Yatra. He said the Centre had no moral right to remain in power after failing to resolve the Ayodhya dispute amicably.

*VHP*

The general secretary of the Indraprastha Vishwa Hindu Parishad, Shri B.L. Sharma, expressed deep regret and indignation over Shri Advani's arrest and warned that those opposing the cause of the Sri Ram mandir whether it be the Janata Dal, the Congress or the Communists will meet the same fate.

*DUSU & ABVP*

Condemnation of Shri Advani's arrest have also come from the university front. While the DUSU vice-president, Shri Awadesh Sharma, charged the Government with overruling the High Court decision and the fundamental right of religion, Shri Raj Kumar Bhatia, national vice-president of the Akhil Bharatiya Vidyarthi Parishad (ABVP) said the Government had not only sought to undermine 'lofty idealist feelings' which Shri Advani's Rath Yatra had aroused but also sought to consolidate its vote bank.

*BMS*

The Bharatiya Mazdoor Sangh condemned the 'forcible stoppage' of the Rath Yatra and the unwarranted arrest of Shri Advani. The BMS advised its members to participate wholeheartedly in the October 24 Bharat bandh.

*Congress-I Leader Shri Romesh Sharma*

A Congress(I) leader Shri Romesh Sharma, said that these were cheap but pernicious game plans to earn political sustenance by some undeserving power hungry groups. The welcoming of Shri Advani's arrests also has come from several quarters.

*IUML*

Stating that the arrest of Shri Advani was correct but belated, Shri Ebrahim Sulaiman Sait, and Shri G.M. Banatwala, president and general secretary respectively of the Indian Union Muslim League appealed to the President of India not to allow the BJP to create a constitutional breakdown.

They have also urged the Government that the repeal of the Ram Janmabhoomi-Babri Masjid ordinance must be with specific provision that the all actions taken under, and the effects of the ordinance are abated and the position prior to the ordinance is fully restored.

*Akali Dal (L)*

The Delhi State Akali Dal (L) general secretary Jathedar Kanwal Kuldeep Singh Bindra welcomed Shri Advani's arrest and emphasised that had Shri Advani not been arrested there was a big possibility of widespread communal disturbances during the Rath Yatra in Uttar Pradesh.

*BMM*

The Bandhua Mukti Morcha leader Swami Agnivesh welcomed Shri Advani's arrest and congratulated the Bihar Chief Minister, Shri Laloo Prasad Yadav, for showing courage to stop the Rath Yatra from proceeding further.

The speech of the Prime Minister on Doordarshan on October 24, 1990 has also evoked varied reactions from different sections of society. In a joint statement issued by some intellectuals under the aegis of Prajna Bharati, the Prime Minister's statements have come in for criticism, specially the portion where he stated *inter alia* that the construction of the Ram temple would lead to the foundation of a theocratic State. "Such a statement coming from India's Prime Minister will mislead and confuse the nation about the Hindu community and the values it propagates".

(*Hindu*, October 24, 1990)

*N. Sanjiva Reddy*

The Former President, Shri N. Sanjiva Reddy, said on October 23, 1990 that the arrest of Shri Advani was 'unfortunate'.

The Ram Janmabhoomi-Babri Masjid issue is an issue of national importance and the BJP has forced the hands of the Government. There is no alternative for the Prime Minister and the Bihar Chief Minister except to prevent him (Shri Advani), from proceeding further in his Rath Yatra".

Shri Reddy said: "It is unfortunate that this (arrest) has taken place. I know Shri Advani and Shri Vajpayee and they are fine people. If everything was left to them, they would have solved this problem".

(*Hindu*, October 24, 1990)

*Sadhu Samaj*

Swami Harinarayan Anand, the general secretary of Bharat Sadhu Samaj, an all-India organisation of ascetic order, expressed regret over the arrest of Shri L.K. Advani, for performing the Rath Yatra to restore an 'ancient temple'.

In a press communique issued on Oct. 23, 1990 he said that there was no 'justification' for the arrest, since the Supreme Court had rejected the plea to ban the programme. The Samaj has called upon the people to maintain peace and communal harmony.

(*Indian Express*, October 24, 1990)

**Withdrawal of BJP Support to NF Government**

Text of the letter submitted by Bharatiya Janata Party. Parliamentary Party leader Atal Behari Vajpayee to President R. Venkataraman. withdrawing support to the National Front Government led by Shri V.P. Singh.

Date 23.10.1990.

To the President of India

Respected Rashtrapatiji,

In view of the multiple failures of the Government, (vide BJP resolution dated 17th instant, copy enclosed) culminating in forcibly preventing the construction of Ram Janmabhoomi mandir and the arrest of our president Shri L.K. Advani, the Bharatiya Janata Party, in pursuance of that resolution, hereby withdraws support from Shri V.P. Singh's Government.

Yours faithfully,

Sd/-

(A.B. Vajpayee)

(*Hindustan Times*, October 24. 1990)

## Reaction to BJP Support Withdrawal

*Chandra Shekhar*

The senior Janata Dal leader, Shri Chandra Shekhar, said on October 23, 1990 the BJP withdrawal of support to the government had created such a "fluid situation" that it was difficult to say if it would necessarily result in the fall of the National Front Government.

Talking to newsmen, Shri Shekhar, who is an arch critic of the Prime Minister, Shri V.P. Singh, said the situation would clear only after three to four days, when the issue is debated the discussed at the ruling party meeting likely to be called shortly.

Although nobody said it in so many words, the feeling in the dissidents' camp, headed by Shri Chandra Shekhar, was that once the Janata Dal elected a new leader in place of Shri V.P. Singh, who has failed to carry with him, the allies of the Dal and thus precipitated the crisis, all the problems would be over.

The dissidents were optimistic that even the BJP could be made to reconsider its stand or a government headed by another leader formed with a possible realignment of political forces.

But Shri Shekhar, himself, was evasive when he was asked a direct question about the possibility of his emerging as the new Prime Minister with the support of other parties or because of likely split in the Janata Dal. "How can I answer such a hypothetical question. It is mainly for the party to decide the issue," he said. Asked about the date of the party meeting, he said: "I don't know. Such questions should be addressed to the party president, Shri S.R. Bommai.

However, the dissidents' leader admitted that he had been busy for the past few days because of the crisis created by the government's failure to carry with it one of its main supporting parties — the BJP. He said he had telephonic talks with Shri Bommai and several other leaders, including the Orissa Chief Minister, Shri Biju Patnaik. Even Shri Bhairon Singh Shekhawat, the Rajasthan Chief Minister, had spoken to him on the phone, he added.

In contrast to the restraint showed by Shri Shekhar in his remarks, the staunch supporters including Shri Yashwant Sinha, Shri Kamal Morarka and Shri Harmohan Dhawan, all MPs, were fortnight in their denunciation of the Prime Minister. They said the Prime Minister ought to have resigned immediately after the withdrawal of support to his government by the BJP. Since has government had lost majority support in the Lok Sabha, the President should not have allowed him to continue, they argued.

They said even if Shri Bommai failed to convene a meeting of the parliamentary party, 10 per cent members of the Janata Dal parliamentary group could demand this meeting, according to the party constitution. Should the things not work out as they desire, apparently, they would invoke the party constitution's provision for calling this meeting, it is learnt.

Shri Yashwant Sinha said the dissidents had not decided how they would go about the issue right now, put they were actually aware of the urgency of the situation. Shri Sinha and the other dissidents said the government has made a mistake in ordering the arrest of Shri Advani. The situation should have been handled more tactfully and without causing annoyance to BJP, they maintained. Asked about the various possibilities in the present situation, Shri Sinha said the Janata Dal would have to sit in the opposition or face the polls.

The dissident MPs repeated that mishandling of the situation was responsible for the crisis facing the government. They maintained the situation had been allowed to drift to such an extent that it had got out of hand, posing a major problem not only for the party but for the whole country.

Shri Chandra Shekhar, voiced his opposition to any mid-term poll as the country could ill-afford general elections within one year.

On the idea of formation of a national government, Shri Chandra Shekhar said that if it had to come about, it could not be "minus anybody". What was needed for a national government was a national perspective about problems facing the nation and commonality of views on how to go about solving them. "A few individuals getting together to share power is not my idea of a national government," he remarked.

Asked to comment on the Congress, he said it was a major political party and one could not wish it away.

(*Times of India*, October 24, 1990)

*Janata Party (JP) Working President*

The Janata Party (JP) working president, Dr. Subramaniam Swamy, said on October 23, 1990 any chance given to the Prime Minister, Shri V.P. Singh, to prove his majority after the withdrawal of the BJP support would "lead to horse trading".

In a statement here, Dr. Swamy demanded that Shri Singh should resign immediately.

He urged the President, Shri R. Venkataraman, to dismiss the V.P. Singh government and invite other leaders to examine the majority support and form the government.

(*Times of India*, October 24, 1990)

### Congress-I Memo to the President

The Congress-I demanded "necessary action" by the President in view of the Prime Minister, Shri V.P. Singh, losing moral, legal and constitutional right" to continue in office.

A 12-member delegation of the Congress-I led by the former External Affairs Minister, Shri P.V. Narasimha Rao, called on the President and submitted a memorandum.

The memorandum expressed the party's "emphatic view" that Shri V.P. Singh, by his gross mismanagement during the last 11 months had brought the nation to the brink of disaster.

Immediately after the nearly half an hour meeting, Shri Narasimha Rao told newsmen that the President was holding necessary consultations to deal with the situation.

Shri Rao declined to comment on what the future course of action of the Congress(I) would be, considering that it is the single largest party in the Lok Sabha with a strength of 195.

A decision to meet the President was taken after an emergency meeting of the Political Affairs Committee of the party and AICC(I) office bearers presided by the party President, Shri Rajiv Gandhi.

(*Financial Express*, October 24, 1990)

### Majority Support in Parliament : Claim by NF

*Prime Minister V.P. Singh*

The Prime Minister, Shri V.P. Singh, met the President for 20 minutes at the Rashtrapati Bhavan after the BJP delegation had an audience with Shri Venkataraman.

Later, talking to newspersons, he said the factual position was that the BJP had withdrawn its support. "But that does not mean that I have lost all support."

Shri Singh apprised the President of the circumstances under which he had agreed to review the ordinance of October 19 regarding the takeover of the disputed land at Ayodhya.

Shri Singh held consultations with his Cabinet and party colleagues and other leaders to take stock of the political situation.

According to official sources, the meeting of the Cabinet as well as the Cabinet Committee on Political Affairs were called to consider the

Government's options to meet the situation.

In a telecast Shri V.P. Singh said the issues arising our of the withdrawal of the BJP support to the Government would be put before Parliament so that the country could see who was standing on which side.

This was essential as basic principles were in question, the Prime Minister said "it is not the question of Government but of principles. The question is whether the Constitution, judiciary and secularism will be upheld or not", he said.

The Prime Minister said it was time for all those who upheld these values, whether they were in politics or social field, to decide whether the country should be run with love and affection or by force and hatred.

He appealed to the people that at this hour they should protect each other as brothers. "At this tense moment my heart goes to the innocent children, men and women who are under tension and under fear", he said.

(*Hindu*, October 24, 1990)

*Janata Dal President S.R. Bommai*

Janata Dal President S.R. Bommai said on October 23, 1990 that the withdrawal of the support by the Bharatiya Janata Party did not "automatically" mean that the Government had lost majority and until the Government had lost the majority in Parliament, it would continue.

Talking to newsmen, he said he expected members of the Lok Sabha to vote according to their conscience when the question of majority comes before Parliament. "We seek the support of all members of Parliament,' Shri Bommai said.

He said the withdrawal of the BJP support had created a "grave political situation" but there was no "crisis". The party, he said, was united and was "unanimous" on the choice of its leader — Shri V.P. Singh. Asked whether the Government would try to stay in power with the Congress-I help, he said, "preposterous".

(*Hindustan Times*, October 24, 1990)

**Reaction to PM's Stand**

*Congress-I*

The Prime Minister, Shri V.P. Singh, was like a "limpet" sticking to his chair even after the BJP had withdrawn its support to the National

Front government, the Congress spokesman, Shri V.N. Gadgil, said.

Stating that the overwhelming view was that the Prime Minister must step down from office at the earliest, Shri Gadgil said the Congress delegation which called on the President, Shri R. Venkataraman, after seeking an urgent appointment with him had underscored the importance of not allowing Shri Singh to delay summoning of the Parliament to prove his majority.

Shri Gadgil expressed confidence that Shri Singh would not be able to wean away any of the Congress MPs to enable him to continue in power. "Our MPs know that if a mid-term poll is held, the Congress has an extremely good chance to securing a handsome mandate from the Indian electorate which wants stability and unity of the country", he stated.

Wondering from where Shri Singh would produce his majority in the Lok Sabha, Shri Gadgil said that the Prime Minister should have displayed dignity and grace by quiting office following the BJP's withdrawal of support.

Replying to questions on the Congress response to the withdrawal of the Ayodhya ordinance. Shri Gadgil said there was hardly any need for any comment. "The National Front government has been transferred from the intensive care ward to the terminal ward", he remarked.

To another question, he said that the BJP and Shri L.K. Advani were the greatest danger to national unity. That is why the Congress Working Committee had demanded that the government stop Shri Advani and his yatra.

(Asked as to the stand of his party on the current political crisis, Shri Gadgil said that Shri Rajiv Gandhi had already made known the party position, reports PTI.

Shri Gandhi stated in Bhagalpur that his party would give constructive cooperation to any government from outside which did not have the BJP and Shri V.P. Singh in it.)

Shri Gadgil released the appeal made by the Congress President, Shri Rajiv Gandhi, which called on the people to maintain peace and harmony and that though the challenges before the country were great, they could be overcome with unity and harmony.

"The events of the last few weeks have caused untold misery to the people of India. There is a fear of communal and caste conflagration. Today we have received some reports of clashes and riots and increased tension and insecurity in certain parts of the country.

(*Times of India*, October 24, 1990)

*Left Parties*

The CPI, CPI-M and other Left parties supported the stand taken by Prime Minister V.P. Singh that he would like to prove on the floor of the Parliament that he still commanded the support of the majority of the members of Parliament.

The Prime Minister refused to resign and took this stand in the wake of the withdrawal of support by the Bharatiya Janata Party to his Government.

In fact, the idea of making this request to President R. Venkataraman emerged at the meeting Shri Singh . . . with the leaders of the Left parties soon after the news came about the BJP's formal move to withdraw support to the National Front Government as a sequel to the arrest of Shri L.K. Advani in Bihar.

The CPI-M is of the assessment that the Congress-I, which is the single largest party in the Lok Sabha, would under compulsion of political events, support the V.P. Singh Government when such a test came in Parliament. CPI-M leader Harkishen Singh Surjeet said that the Congress-I would be politically isolated if it acted otherwise.

According to party sources, West Bengal Chief Minister Jyoti Basu was reported to have made this point to Shri Rajiv Gandhi. This information was believed to have been given by Shri Basu at a meeting of party colleagues in Calcutta. The expectation in CPI-M circles was that Shri Gandhi would make a positive response to the plea.

In fact, Shri Surjeet said there would be other occasions later when the Congress-I could settle scores with Shri Singh or his Government. But here was a moment when all secular and democratic parties would be on test, and political wisdom demanded that at this critical juncture, the Congress-I supported the V.P. Singh Government on this specific issue.

Expectations in the Chandrashekhar camp, however were different. One Janata Dal leader who openly canvassed for a change in leadership of the party, hoped that the Left parties would support Shri Chandrashekhar it he was elected as the new leader of the Janata Dal Parliamentary Party in place of Shri Singh.

The CPI-M spokesman, however, discounted all such speculations and said they were not concerned with these formulations and urged the JD leaders to concentrate on the bigger challenges ahead — of communal tensions and riots created by Shri Advani's Rath Yatra.

The Left parties, in their joint statement, warned that the BJP might engineer more communal disturbances in the country to protest against the arrest of Shri Advani.

The CPI-M leaders, however, recognised that at the moment, the V.P. Singh Government faced instability as a result of the withdrawal of support by the BJP and felt that other secular parties, like the Left parties, should support Shri Singh to meet the grave challenge in the interest of the unity of the country. . . .

CPI leader Shri M. Farooqi also felt that this was not the time to entertain the idea of change in leadership of the party. The CPI, like other Left parties, reaffirmed its support to Shri Singh to meet the crisis. . . .

The Left parties, in their joint statement, urged the Government to maintain law and order "at all costs" and "nip in the bud" any attempts at disturbing communal harmony in the country. They blamed the BJP for "instigating" the people by giving a call for a Bharat bandh and added that the situation needed vigilance, both by the people and the Government.

(*Hindustan Times*, October 24, 1990)

*JNU Teachers*

The Janata Dal Parliamentary Party should now meet and elect another leader, for the Bharatiya Janata Party has withdrawn its support to the V.P. Singh Government, but it has not said that it has withdrawn its support to the Janata Dal as such, said three eminent professors of Jawaharlal Nehru University in a statement on October 23, 1990..

Professor M.L. Sondhi, Professor Parimal Kumar Das and Professor Devendra Kaushik suggested that both the sides can now enter into a special consultation in order to make a transition to a new Prime Minister as smooth as possible.

They said Shri V.P. Singh's initiative to continue in Government after losing the support of the BJP can only mean that he is going to join hands with the Congress(I), a step which can hardly make him the champion and protector of value-based politics. Even on the basis of the most favourable prognosis of Leftist support, Shri V.P. Singh cannot compensate for the last and fatal blunder of Shri Advani's arrest.

His dependence on Shri Rajiv Gandhi's support will mean forsaking all standards of integrity in public life. The effort to manipulate public opinion by creating a veneer of morality will deceive no one.

It is therefore inevitable and proper that Shri V.P. Singh should immediately step down and the Janata Dal should elect a new leader who should show a good deal more common sense in dealing with senior leaders like Shri Advani and in defusing crises instead of aggravating them.

The President, Shri R. Venkataraman, would be well advised to ignore both Shri V.P. Singh and Shri Rajiv Gandhi's calculations and take account of the discernible element of popular consent which led to the enlarged representation of the Janata Dal and the BJP in the Lok Sabha. He cannot be guided by the unproved assumptions of either Shri V.P. Singh or Shri Rajiv Gandhi. He must also order the immediate release of Shri Advani and thereby favourably change the climate of opinion in the country, the three academicians said.

In another joint statement four eminent writers and commentators, Shri Nikhil Chakravarty, Editor, Mainstream, Prof. Rajni Kothari, a member of the Planning Commission, Dr. George Mathew, Director of the Institute of Social Sciences, and Shri O.V. Vijayan "greeted" the firm decision of the National Front Government to stop the "Rath Yatra".

They said India's secular and democratic credentials have been under strain by the brazen attempts at mixing political ambition with religious emotions. The Government has stood this test with patience and we are confident that the people will remain true to the country's established tradition of respect for one another's religious faith. It does democracy no good if a few groups are allowed, on whatever grounds, to take the law into their hands, instead of settling issues through argument and negotiation, with restraint and maturity.

"India has come a long way since the post-Partition communal holocaust; and we believe that the experience since then of people of differing persuasions working peacefully together, often under trying conditions, towards shared social goals, has already created a forward momentum that will not be easily reversed. And we urge the Government, all political parties and the people of India to turn the challenge facing us at this critical time into an opportunity to transcend the sectarian divisions and strengthen the integrity of the country and of our democracy," they said.

(*Statesman*, October 24, 1990)

*Union Minister of State Maneka Gandhi Resigns in Protest*

Text of Mrs Maneka Gandhi's letter:

October 26, 1990

Dear Prime Minister

As you are well aware, I have been very unhappy at the strange unilateral decisions taken by you in the last few months. These decisions not only relate to my area of work but also to all matters of governance. These include: Yet another postponement of elections in Punjab, — the refusal to deal expeditiously with the victims of the 1984 massacre and subsequent terrorism, – the lack of a coherent policy on Kashmir and the lack of clear thinking on how this state should be governed, — the complete refusal to recognise the oil crisis even though it was looming for months, and the shortsighted measures that have been taken to deal with it.

These have resulted only in inflation of prices, not in tackling the problem.

— The peculiar manner in which you have chosen to ignore the over-whelming circumstantial evidence on the Bofors case despite the fact that you have the facts with you for some time.

— The hasty and unthought through manner in which parts of the Mandal report were sought to be implemented bringing no relief to the poor and backward and unnecessarily adding to the miseries of our youth.

Sir, there is no such thing as 'the management of contradictions'. "There is truth and there is untruth, and they cannot be managed or even reconciled. We made several simple easily fulfillable promises to the people of India when we sought their vote. These revolved round honesty and efficiency in Government.

I have tried my best to live up to these two ideals under the most trying circumstances created by you. But I really do believe that we have now reached an impasse.

We are in a minority. We were always that but we were accepted on the basis of certain values that we professed to bring into Indian politics. Staying in power as a minister for a few days longer merely to horsetrade is not my idea of these values or of politics.

Therefore I resign. i believe that you too should step down in the interests of the same morality we hold so dear.

Thank you for giving me the opportunity to serve in your Government.

Yours Sincerely,
Maneka Gandhi
(*Indian Express*, October 27, 1990)

## Press Views

*Uncertain Times*

The inherent contradictions in the National Front Government, which was supported from the outside by the BJP on the one hand, and the Left parties on the other, have reached their inevitable denouement . . . stand taken by the BJP over the Ram Janmabhoomi issue, and the government's. . . response to it, which culminated in the arrest of Shri L.K. Advani, have led to the withdrawal of support by the BJP. Ordinarily, this ought to signify the end of the V.P. Singh government. But it speaks volumes for the sort of culture that has come to dominate Indian politics that thoughts have automatically turned to what is termed as a 'realignment of political force' — a euphemism for horse-trading and wheeling-dealing of the worst sort. It is not surprising, therefore, that Shri V.P. Singh has decided to stay put until he can prove (and he will surely need a miracle to help him out) his majority on the floor of the house. Of course, he is well within his rights in acting as he has done. On the other hand, one cannot help recalling the conduct of Shri Morarji Desai, who when he realised that he had lost the majority in the Lok Sabha, decided to go, and not stay. The prospect that faces the country now is one of tremendous uncertainty until the next general election. For, even if Shri Singh or his successor manages to cobble together a majority of sorts. It is certain not to last the full term. The inherent contradictions are too many. The sitting MP's will not, of course, want to face the electorate a bare 11 months after having been elected, and most of them would probably prefer to hang on for as long as is possible. But the self-interest of MP's cannot be equated with the national interest, and the sooner the ninth Lok Sabha makes way for the tenth, the better it will be for the country.

(Editorial, *Economic Times*, October 24, 1990)

*What of the Nation?*

The events of the past week are quite regrettable. There can be no better description of the developments that have taken place in the wake of the BJP's resolve to go ahead with the Rath Yatra. Shri Advani's arrest was inevitable, . . . leading to his party withdrawing support to the National Front Government. The situation is not entirely tailor-made for the return of the Congress(I) to power at the Centre. Still, if Mr V.P. Singh goes out, what is the alternative? A mid-term poll no political party might like, neither for that matter the voter. It is no use blaming the National Front for not providing stability. A minority Government critically dependent on outside support cannot go on for long and it will be a miracle if Shri Singh survives this latest threat,. . . his manner of governance and the measures he adopted, particularly his acceptance of the Mandal Commission recommendations, are not reassuring. People have reason to worry about the consequences of these rash measures and now we have the Rath Yatra and the controversy surrounding the temple at Ayodhya. We had. . . strongly advocated letting both the temple and the mosque be in the disputed territory. This still remains the only workable remedy to the kind of situation that we are facing. Politicians have no right to blow up a trivial matter into a serious communal dispute. The BJP may have got its electoral calculations right, but this is no time to angle for the Hindu vote. The party still does not have much following beyond the Vindhyas. The Congress (I) itself was reduced to a regional party over successive elections and after the 1989 defeat it, perhaps, is only a sub-regional party. The BJP which wants to acquire considerable influence at the national level must learn from the Congress (I)'s discomfiture. It has to grow into a truly national party cutting across state boundaries. It must cease to be a Hindu party. It has to enjoy the support of the minorities.

(Editorial, *Financial Express*, October 24, 1990)

*What lies Ahead?*

Perhaps lulled into a sense of security by the success of the triangular experiment, the National Front Government in recent months embarked on an ambitious programme of political and social mobilisation, the most high profile instance of which was the implementation of the nearly forgotten Mandal recommendations. Driven to this policy course by a sense of being besieged by internal pressure and the lack of an enduring political base, the V.P. Singh Government chose to step outside the realm of consensual decision taking, which had been the style of its earlier phase. The BJP's amiability vanished as it felt that its own base was likely to be fractured by the Government's new political tactics and strategy. The post-Mandal context saw a rapid souring of the atmosphere between the BJP and the National Front, with the Ayodhya controversy becoming the flashpoint. On the Ramjanmabhoomi issue, both had lacked themselves into irreconcilable and rigid stances. The National Front had, by the logic of its own political circumstances and in response to the key task of governance of this sharply variegated polity, perforce to take upon itself the task of defending the political principle of secularism. . . .

What lies ahead? In the immediate context, confusion — as the leading political players try to assess the situation, their own chances of staking power and the various permutations and combinations that can yield an enduring majority. It is certainly a situation without precedent, the nearest parallel perhaps being 1979. And it is the President who will have to decide which option would be constitutionally correct and politically viable. It will be no easy decision to take, given the shape of the present Parliament, where no single party can be certain of commanding majority support at all times. Much will depend on the internal dynamics of the various groups staking their claims, the integrity of the ruling National Front parliamentary party and the attitude of the largest single party — the Congress (I). It remains to be seen whether the momentum of recent developments are pushing things in the direction of a realignment of political forces, if not immediately, perhaps a little later. But what is of real urgency is to find a governing arrangement or structure that will have enough stability to respond to the increasingly complex and critical scenario facing the country. Unfortunately, there is at present an atmosphere of restiveness and a sense of deepening social divide, even as the polity's wounds in Kashmir and Punjab continue to fester. Therefore, the decision as to whether the National Front Government must be given another chance to prove its case that it retains a majority, or whether some time must be given to allow an alternative leader or coalition to emerge, or whether to go back to the polls, must be primarily guided by just one thing. And it is this: a sense of urgency to restore political stability at the Centre so that the country may be governed by a team of persons that will not waste its time on the kind of games of one-upmanship that we have been watching for some months now but will concentrate its energies on building a cohesive society.

(Editorial, *Hindu*, October 24, 1990)

*The Crisis*

The inevitable has happened. The country has been pushed into a political crisis by thoughtless men whose job was to manage its affairs at a critical juncture. At every step they have been matching each other's skill to complicate the issues and fight battles that could be avoided. Not one among the present set of available leaders on the scene has risen above narrow considerations, personal or partisan.

The crisis over Shri Om Prakash Chautala earlier this year, Shri V.P. Singh's attempt to carve out a support base by resorting to the Mandal Commission and Shri L.K. Advani's attempt to look for votes for his party in the name of religion have all led to the present crisis. Shri Advani's arrest at Samastipur was the culmination of a process that had set in much earlier. The way events are taking shape and a pack of short-sighted men is pushing the country further on a disastrous course can only deepen the anxiety of the people.

Shri V.P. Singh ought to have known that his decision on the Mandal Report was bad in law and spirit and was a product of electoral motivations. He should have known that it would divide an already fractured society and alienate an entire constituency that creatively used could take the society ahead and work at the same time for distributive justice for the deprived. He chose a different track and the country is paying for it. . . .

The present crisis is also linked with politics of the Janata Dal leaders and so far they have not changed their leader although the party's dissidents are active, hoping for the worst for Shri V.P. Singh. The Janata Dal members must make up their mind at the earliest one way or the other so that Parliament has less complications on its hand when it decides the fate of the V.P. Singh Government — i.e. if it is given an opportunity by the President to do so.

Whatever the developments during the next couple of days, it is too clear the country is heading for a mid-term poll. Dissolution of Parliament in any case has to accompany in case the President chooses to ask Shri V.P. Singh to quit. And permission to Shri V.P. Singh to test his majority can throw up no different proposition either.

Also, the withdrawal of the BJP's support from Shri V.P. Singh marks the failure of the second experiment to evolve an alternative to the Congress Party. Ten years ago such an experiment floundered when the Janata Party leaders could not sort out their quarrels; now the Janata Dal's inner quarrels and conflicting ambitions have led to a situation that again seems to be marking another failure of a major attempt to throw up an alternative to the Congress. In any case, a mid-term poll is likely to be preceded by re-alignment of the forces and search for new political constituencies. There are many possibilities in the situation. May be new coalitional arrangements will emerge out of the present crisis.

(Editorial, *Hindustan Times*, October 24, 1990)

*Inescapable Consequences*

V.P. Singh, who has in the past made it a practice to resign when there has been no reason to do so, has declared that he will not resign, now that there is every reason for him to do so. The BJP has withdrawn support but that does not mean I don't have supporters, he says, I will prove my strength when Parliament meets. And that could be a month hence.

There is a self-image in all this, as well as calculation. V.P. Singh plans to play at being Caesar so that everyone sees him being stabbed in the Senate and some Antony proclaims him a martyr to great principles — uplift of the poor, secularism. He hopes meanwhile to garner the support of the "backward caste" and Muslim MPs from several parties, he hopes too to capitalise on the difficulties that the Janata Dal will have in settling on an alternative leader, and on the apparent decision of the Congress (I) to stay out of government so that the mess worsens and the disgust with its opponents becomes unshakable. . . .

Some legacy that V.P. Singh leaves!

The last act — The *Rath Yatra* and the eventual arrest of L.K. Advani — too will have far-reaching consequences. The *Yatra* itself and even more so the tumultuous response at evoked were a reaction to an entire pattern of politics — of appeasing the *thekedars* of the minorities. the manner in which V.P. Singh somersaulted in the end — not once but thrice in two days — to the dictates of Imam Bukhari and the rest was one of the most dramatic, if also one of the most craven instances yet of this brand of politics. The sequence will therefore further fan Hindu reaction. If only our politicians, and even more so our pseudo-secularists, saw the wind they sow.

(Editorial, *Indian Express*, October 24, 1990)

. . . if the BJP was allowed to carry out its outrageous plan to take over the disputed shrine and mount a direct assault on the Babri Masjid, it might have signalled the end of much that is of value to Indian society — the rule of law, the principle of respect for all religions and the ideal of a common motherland of all communities. But the danger is not yet over,. . . the BJP might now retaliate by becoming even more communal. . . . The need is all the greater,. . . but because there is no dearth of parties which might use this opportunity to settle personal scores rather than join forces to fight the sectarian virus. The BJP's problem, of course, is that having burnt its boats so far as its former secular allies are concerned, it feels unable to turn back. It is to be hoped that the innate good sense of the Indian people will ensure that its future "Yatra" will be towards the isolated fringe of national politics where it has always belonged.

(Editorial, *Statesman*, October 25, 1990)

Unfortunately however, the National Front Government is now bereft of the legitimacy it requires to enforce the writ of the state. The withdrawal of the BJP's support leaves Shri V.P. Singh without a requisite majority in Parliament. As is his wont the Prime Minister has refused to acknowledge this plain reality. He appears to be in no hurry at all to secure a vote of confidence in his government. Yet, the more he drags his feet in the matter the more he risks creating an altogether unprecedented Constitutional crisis which is bound to jeopardize the government's efforts to deal with the fall-out of Shri Advani's arrest. To dispel the impression that he is engaged in unseemly horse-trading in order to continue in office, Shri Singh must lose no time to convene Parliament at the earliest. If he fails to win a vote of confidence, President Venkataraman will be free to exercise his prerogatives.

Shri V.P. Singh cannot for a moment forget that at the moment his is a lame-duck government and that he himself is a care-taker Prime Minister. Instead of seeking Constitutional loop-holes to be able to continue in office it is incumbent on him to swiftly end the instability at the Centre. A weak Centre, whose very legitimacy is now in doubt, is in no position at all to face the awesome problems now plaguing the country. Therefore, any step he takes to cut short the political uncertainty in the Capital is certain to redound to his credit. . . by projecting the image of a Prime Minister who resorts to base stratagems to cling to power. Indeed if the abdicates office at this stage without even waiting to secure a vote confidence in his government, there is every reason to believe that he will enhance his reputation. Meanwhile, a word is also in order regarding the BJP's responsibility in this hour of crisis. The arrest of Shri L.K. Advani will have served a purpose if it persuades his party's leadership that militant Hinduism is the very antithesis of Indian nationhood. . . . A beginning in this direction can be made in the present Parliament if possible; if not, the wisdom of the electorate should be trusted to bring about such a realignment in the next Parliament.

(Editorial, *Times of India*, October 24, 1990)